AF420578

Praise for *The Hole in Your Life*

Thank you for asking me to read your recent book on grief. Its insights will help countless people struggling with loss. I recently lost my youngest sister, and it was a blessing to read your thoughts on the paths I can take toward remembering her in healthy ways.

Georgiann Baldino, author of twelve fiction and nonfiction books, numerous essays and short stories, and the editor for three nonfiction titles.

Dr Bob Rich's *The Hole in Your Life* is written from the heart. It shares his personal experience and many case studies with his clients, making research-based recommendations on how to process grief in a very readable and easy to apply manner.

Dr David Morawetz, Counselling Psychologist, parent of a child who died, an expert grief counsellor, and Founder and Director, Social Justice Fund

The Hole in Your *Life* will be a tremendous resource for anyone who is ready to seek a path forward after suffering a loss. I hope that anyone going through grief or loss will give your heartfelt words of wisdom a sincere try. As I read this book, I did feel as if a kind grandfather (who happens to be a psychologist) was gently guiding the reader on a loving, practical, and soul-empowering journey to cope with loss and even overcome grief. (I'm not personally grieving, but would love to share this resource with anyone who is.) Grief is something that touches everyone's life at some point or another, so it only makes sense to empower ourselves with the tools to cope - and who better to learn from than Dr. Bob Rich, a psychologist with decades of experience helping patients overcome a wide variety of life's problems, including of course, grief.

I. C. Robledo, a bestselling author and editor in self-development.

The Hole in Your Life is a good toolbox for coping with grief and I agree with all of it. Among the points that resonated with me most deeply are these ideas: grief is part of our life experience, so let's not be afraid of it; it is easier to recover from grief if you grieve before the person dies and suffer with them; and, that only way to learn from loss with meaning is through suffering, as long as it is not self-inflicted.

Alfredo Zotti, author of *Music Therapy: An Introduction with case studies for mental illness recovery.*

After reading this book, I feel I've had some professional development. Great book for practitioners.

Judith Baldacchino, a psychologist with over 30 years of experience.

The Hole in Your Life:

Grief and Bereavement

Bob Rich, PhD

Loving Healing Press

Ann Arbor, MI

The Hole in Your Life: Grief and Bereavement
Copyright © 2025 by Bob Rich, PhD. All rights reserved.

ISBN 979-8-89656-051-7 paperback
ISBN 979-8-89656-052-4 hardcover
ISBN 979-8-89656-053-1 eBook

Published by
Loving Healing Press   Tollfree (888)761-628
5145 Pontiac Trail   info@LHPress.com
Ann Arbor, MI 48105   www.LHPress.com

Distributed by Ingram Book Group (USA, CAN, UK, AU, EU)

Contents

To my darling daughter, Natalie,

who had dedicated her all-too-short life

to being of benefit to others.

Special Online Supplement to
The Hole in Your Heart

Whenever you see an <u>underlined phrase</u> in the book, please go to bobswriting.com/glinks.html

You will discover more than two dozen complementary short pieces in the form of fiction, personal memoir, and self-help vignettes that bring you a deeper understanding of grieving and its nuances.

Natalie

One morning in May 2023, my daughter, Natalie, looked in the mirror to see that the whites of her eyes had turned yellow. Her skin had darkened. Her brother, who lives interstate, happened to phone her, and she told him about her changes as if they were something to laugh about. He said, "See your doctor, NOW!"

The doctor chased her off to a hospital, where they diagnosed her with advanced liver cancer. It was inoperable because it had started in the bile duct.

Nineteen months of medical torture later, she was dead. We are preparing for her funeral as I write, in December 2024.

This book on grief was almost completed, with only three sections waiting to be written, but I'd put it aside. I got it out and decided to make it my next project as part of processing my grief. And as on previous occasions when I've suffered the loss of a loved one, her passing allowed me to field test the many ways of coping with grief I'll share with you.

I'd love to illustrate my daughter's caring nature for you. In Australia, European wasps are a vicious invader species. Nevertheless, I have seen her save one from drowning. "They are living things, so deserve to be helped," she said. She also invested hundreds of hours crocheting beautiful rugs for homeless people, many of whom are older women who live in their cars. Most people avoid a staggering drunk. In contrast, when the two of us were out on one of our enjoyable walks together, she insisted we help one cross a road, then we even escorted him home.

She was stubborn and insisted on having her own way, even from before birth. My wife and I lived on a scholarship and couldn't afford a baby yet. Despite everything medical science could do,

Natalie came along anyway. My wife went into labor, and then the baby stayed inside through 72 hours of contractions, until SHE had made up her mind to face the world.

When she was four years old, she insisted on starting school, and was so adamant that despite the hole it made in our finances, we enrolled her in a private school. One of my favorite photos is the class lined up by order of height. Natalie was on the end, a head shorter than the next shortest kid. But she could count to a thousand, "a THOUSAND, Dad," and was best at all the academic stuff, something she maintained until graduating with a medal.

To conclude this trait, she planned her own funeral, which is to be a Purple Party. Everyone is required to wear something purple. Her sister, Anina, is to speak, and Natalie instructed her and the celebrant, who is a in her nineties but came temporarily out of retirement because she used to be Natalie's client.

Natalie's work was basically that of a small business counselor. Her delight was to save people from bankruptcy, to guide them to a long-term sustainable business, to act with wisdom. Like the celebrant, most of them became devoted friends for life.

As you can see, I love her immensely.

And yet, only days after her passing, I have peace in my heart, can enjoy a joke, and get on with the conduct of life. A typical thought is, "Thank heavens, she is at peace now, and no longer suffering."

If I can do this, then perhaps you can, too, though there are never any guarantees. Everyone's journey through grief is different. The "normal course of grief" usually takes one to two years and may even be longer. It is not a race but, if we make the right choices, it is a way of growing and becoming better people.

Part I
Finding a Path to Healing
A Glimmer of Hope

I hope this little book will be a source of solace and healing for you. After all, why would you read it if you were not grieving?

I will also show you a path to becoming a stronger, wiser, better person after your period of grief. That can be your silver lining, and the way of honoring the memory of those you have lost.

Through the years, I have learned a great deal through formal training, personal experience, and, above all, from my clients. It is my honor and privilege to pass these tools for wellbeing on to you, whatever situation you face.

The COVID-19 pandemic has killed millions. Although not usually added up, the environmental catastrophe we are in has killed even more. There is gun violence, wars, some of which have gone on for decades, the unacknowledged epidemic of cancer... on and on.

This is not to sound a note of gloom, but to remind you that you are not alone. Losing loved ones is part of life and is the natural order of things. However much it hurts, in a sense it is normal. All through the ages, people have lost parents, children, life partners, friends. It may feel as if the terrible times will go on forever, but here is the first survival trick: step outside yourself for a moment and look around. If other people could somehow resolve their grief and be able to build a good life for themselves, then chances are you will, too, however impossible it may feel now.

Breaking a leg is a good analogy. It hurts, terribly. If all goes well, six weeks later the bone will have healed, and actually be stronger at the point of break than elsewhere. There may be complications such as an infection, so there are no guarantees, but mostly, life eventually goes on.

Grief is the emotional reaction to a loss. It can last a minute for having lost a friendly game, or for the rest of your life for the worst loss you can imagine: feeling guilt for the death of your child. One of the greatest joys of my career was being of service to a couple who had suffered this tragedy.

We'll call them Margaret and Jim. They'd married two years before, but now both had returned to live with their parents, and sold their house and its contents. They were referred by two different doctors for being suicidal. When I found out they were a separated couple, I offered to refer one of them on, but both had specifically asked for me because of recommendations from ex-clients. I saw them individually for nine sessions each, then three more sessions with them together.

I won't describe their tragedy, because it is guaranteed to trigger trauma for many readers. Let us just say that she was a little negligent, and he was a little careless, and as a direct result their toddler son died in a horrific way.

Later on, I'll describe the tools that helped them, including what the three of us invented. For now, since even they could resolve their grief and emerge at the other end fully functioning, there is hope for you.

The Goal

Successfully resolving grief is not a matter of forgetting or replacing the person you have lost. Nothing will ever do that. People and even animals who have had a special place in your heart will stay there as long as you live. In time, though, if all goes well, the memory will usually be free of pain, and even involve a smile, or laughter when recalling a funny event.

There may be special days when the tears will come: typical are birthdays, anniversaries, and celebrations like Christmas. On these days, set aside time to honor the memory. This can be by yourself, or a shared ceremony with others who love the same person. Please read this little story: "A Different Christmas Tale.*"

Alone or in a group, get out old photographs, bring to mind stories from back-then: all the good times, stories of this person's influence into shaping you into who you have become, jokes and misunderstandings and so on. This is a "Remember when..." event. And yes, even a departed child or pet will have had an influence on your current way of being.

Natalie had a special ceremony of remembrance like this on the anniversary of the death of her cat, Leo.

For the rest of the year, life should go on, with perhaps weeks or even months without thinking of the dead person, but sometimes this can be several times a day, as appropriate reactions to events around you. We once had a dear friend who loved to serve up drinks that were HEALTHY for you. They were, but sour enough to convert your mouth into a tightly closed purse. So, when we bite

---

* Remember, each time you see an underlined phrase, please visit **bobswriting.com/glinks.html** for fiction, personal memoir, and self-help vignettes that bring you a deeper understanding of grieving and its nuances.

into a fruit that proves a little sour, we refer to it as "a Beth." This gives us a grin, and is a perfectly good way to remember her.

My wife and I regularly play a game while sharing a meal. This is "hoppity board," a more complex version of Chinese checkers. My mother-in-law also used to enjoy this game but had a habit of picking up a marble and waving it around, then forgetting (or perhaps pretending to forget) which hole it came from. So, in my family, a class of actions is referred to as "doing a Mother," always with a fond laugh. The other day, I lost a sock and looked for it everywhere. It eventually turned up in the pocket of my trousers, of all places. This was "doing a Mother."

After the grief is gone, though the memory and loving stays, you will feel free to give the same love to new people. Widows and widowers may marry again. Parents of dead children can raise new ones. Even children of departed parents can adopt honorary parents. I have a "daughter" who has lost three parents: her mother died, eventually father remarried, then father died, then (beloved) stepmother, too. She became best friends at university with my daughter, Anina, and one day announced that she decided to adopt us as her new mother and father.

I assume that reaching this state feels impossible for you at this time. But, like that broken bone, an injury takes time to heal. As I've said, serious grief may take over two years to resolve. Remember that, and when you can, keep the goal in mind.

Scheduling: Immediate First Aid

Rose had nursed her husband at home through three years of cancer, and then he died. She had a responsible job, but three months later found herself still making mistakes. An unkind colleague delighted in "helpfully" pointing them out to her, and voiced the opinion that after three months, surely she was over it.

Well, no. That would be quite unusual.

Rose sought counseling after driving through a red light on two occasions. You see, until he got too ill, her husband was the invariable driver when they went out together. So, she'd be sitting at the wheel, thinking, *John should be driving*, and collapsed inside, with no attention left for anything else.

She and I together invented a tool I have used myself, and taught to hundreds of clients. It is useful for any all-consuming thought or worry, not only grief.

In her appointment diary, she wrote "John" for 5-7 pm, seven days a week. During those two hours, she gave herself permission to feel whatever she needed to feel, do whatever she needed to do. She could cry, rage at the unfairness of it all, or whatever else was necessary at her current state of grieving.

Any other time, like at work or driving, she reacted to a thought of grief by saying within her mind, *Go away, love, I'll talk to you at five o'clock.*

This worked remarkably well for Rose, for me, and for everyone else who has given it an honest go. As long as you meticulously keep the appointment, the grief (or other consuming worry) is willing to wait for it.

Grief needs to be experienced. It needs to be felt—but not 24 hours a day. At first, like Rose did, devote two hours a day to it.

Later, this can be gradually reduced, so at a certain point it might be half an hour every Sunday, or, as I said, eventually only on special days of remembrance.

It is a good idea to separate your scheduled grief period from your usual bedtime by a few hours, otherwise it can be whenever it is convenient.

Journaling

I am a writer and think in words. So, one of the natural activities during my scheduled grieving times has been a free-flow recording of my emotions, thoughts, motivations (or lack of them) as part of grieving. This works for grief, anticipatory grief, and any other emotional tyrant wanting to rob you of sleep, of joy, of life even.

I started a grief journal when Natalie was diagnosed, which means that I had nineteen months of grief processing when she died. This is probably one of the reasons I am functioning well enough to surprise myself, only weeks after her passing. Further along, I'll discuss two more reasons.

A Love Story: The Transformative Power of the Twelve Steps by Nancy Oelklaus is about alcoholism and family secrets, but is also the account of how a wise woman dealt with the death of her husband, which had triggered her grief for her father. Her main tool was journaling: writing down her thoughts as they came to her, at first daily, then as appropriate. About half of this little book is excerpts from her journal.

Similarly, *Hummingbird: Messages from My Ancestors* by Diana Raab includes a beautiful, poetic account of how the author used poetry and journaling to heal from multiple sources of grief.

So, if it suits you, journaling can be an excellent activity during your scheduled times.

The Power of NOW

Thinking only hurts when you do it. You can't switch it off, and trying to do so will only make it stronger, but you can convert it into a meaningless background like the sound of a breeze in the treetops. The training tool for achieving this is mindfulness meditation.

If you already have the skill, use it. If not, this chapter is a mini-instruction manual. Put it into practice. At first, meditate a few minutes at a time. As you get better at it, extend the length.

In addition to formal sessions, you can meditate on occasions like when stopped at a red light, in the waiting room of a doctor or dentist, standing in line at the supermarket, while on hold on the phone (though the stupid music can get in the way, especially if announcements are laced into it).

Ever since I stopped distance running, I have been slow to get to sleep. So, I settle myself, then spend half an hour or more meditating. I don't know how long I manage, because I do drift off to sleep somewhere along the line.

OK, how do you do it?

Pick something to focus on. The breath is the most frequent because it is always there and has a special significance, but it could be a candle flame, the back of the person in front of you in the line, the sound of rain on the roof, the smell of dinner cooking, the movement of the muscles in your legs while walking—virtually anything.

In Vipassana meditation, you do a body scan, shifting your focus gradually and systematically over all the body. So, it might be full, 100% focus on your left little toe, then during the next breath the fourth one… all the way to the top of your head. But this advanced skill is unnecessary for our purpose here.

Put all your attention on your chosen focus. Other things are guaranteed to intrude: sounds, movements in your peripheral vision if your eyes are open, an itch, thoughts… The essence of mindfulness meditation is to allow such distractions rather than trying to send them away. As soon as you notice one, thank it, then simply return your attention to your focus. It is perfectly all right to scratch an itch, to take note of a movement or a sound, to acknowledge a thought. Having done so, return. You will find this cycle easier and easier with practice. Once you are good at it, you can improve further by not scratching that itch, or waving at a fly buzzing around your nose, but simply allowing it while you continue to attend to your focus.

And while you are meditating, you are not hurting. It is a holiday from worry, grief, anger, guilt, anxiety, sadness. Those emotions can be there, but because you keep returning your attention to your focus, they stay as background, more and more distant and of less and less importance.

Once this is easy, you can start living mindfully. Use whatever you are doing as the focus. So, this instant, I am writing, which is a complex activity. I need to keep in mind the message of this section, what I want to say in this paragraph, how to word it. Then there are the more mechanical aspects of grammar, spelling, punctuation, touch typing on my keyboard.

This multiple activity is my focus, and it shows that while the object of focus can be unitary like the breath, it can also be complex.

Suppose you are trying to focus on your breath, but your heartbeat keeps intruding into your consciousness. One trick is to include it: the focus can be pulse AND breath. Jon Kabat-Zinn's method for dealing with physical pain is to gently and kindly focus on the unpleasant sensation while also staying aware of the breath: "Say hello to the pain, for this in-breath." Then, with practice, this is extended to make the unpleasant sensation the focus.

Deepak Chopra has described a form of mindfulness meditation in which you keep your awareness on as many different things as possible. He says some people can manage twenty. I can routinely do eight, but it's not a contest, and there is no need to show off. But if some noise keeps pulling you away from your chosen focus, you can add it as something extra to focus on.

Jon Kabatt-Zinn calls focusing on everything around you "living in the *nowscape*." It is a marvelous state when you are able achieve it. I have illustrated it with a cheeky story—but a bit of fun is healthy, whether you are grieving or not. It is "<u>Walking, boring?</u>" And my little essay, "<u>Heaven</u>", shows you what the nowscape feels like.

Let's stop a moment. While you were reading about mindfulness meditation, were you calm? The searchlight of attention was on my words, everything else becoming background.

That's how mindfulness works.

When driving a car, do so with full attention. The focus of your meditation is all of: staying safe, keeping to the correct path and, hopefully, obeying the law.

When weeding your garden, all your attention can be on identifying plants you don't want there, gently but firmly removing them, shaking the soil off the roots... this moment, this instant, THIS is all there is.

Feel the peace.

Next moment, you may lose the peace and suffering may return, but the past is history, the future is a mystery, I give you a present. All that is real is this moment. So, quietly return to living with full focus on this instant, and the peace will return.

To go full circle, do mindfulness meditation whenever you can, and it will build into a haven you carry around with you. This is my second tool for dealing with the recent loss of my daughter.

Part II:
The Nature of Grief

Everyone has heard about Elisabeth Kübler-Ross's description of the stages of grief: denial, anger, bargaining, depression, and acceptance.

If only things were that simple and predictable! But grief is not some clockwork toy mechanically progressing along a preset path. While Elisabeth's model is complex and flexible, she later regretted the way folk wisdom transformed it into a simple recipe that's simply wrong.

No, grief is a savage dragon that rips into you and changes you forever, for good or bad. (And yes, suffering can transform you into a better person.) It follows no set path but ravages each of us in a unique way.

Yes, it starts with "I just can't believe it," but that can return much later, time and again. We can feel furious at the unfairness and lost opportunity of the passing of a young person, years after the grief has been resolved. Even if briefly, acceptance can come early on.

Those five reactions, and many more, form a multidimensional maelstrom of experiences.

I have found Elizabeth Harper Neeld's model of grieving to be more useful. Before I retired, I owned three copies of her book, *Seven Choices: Finding Daylight after Loss Shatters Your World*, and lent a copy to clients needing to recover from a serious loss. But of course, in those days I didn't have this book to lend out, did I?

Elizabeth becomes a friend to every reader of her book. Her story is personal, passionate from the heart, and yet scientifically valid.

She doesn't identify stages, but a back-and-forth, up-and-down process that can progress toward resolution if we make the right choices—or fail to do so if we don't. These are the Seven Choices of the title.

I will now illustrate her seven choice points with real-life stories, sufficiently changing each to protect my clients' privacy. Every person's path through grief is different. Yours will be different from mine, and from my clients', but I am sure you will be able to identify with many of these little stories. As I said at the start, this alone is validation that your feelings are OK, and that there is an excellent chance you will get through them to a better place.

Elizabeth's first choice point is **Impact**.

Gabrielle was a Victims of Crime client. The referral stated the dry facts: Her son was attending a wedding. When he came outside, he saw two men molesting a young woman and went to her aid. A third man approached from behind and punched the back of his head. He died in the ambulance on the way to the hospital.

We had our first session a week later. Gabrielle's eyes were clear, face calm, body relaxed. In a business-like way she said, "Oh, I've been so busy, organizing the funeral, and my daughter-in-law has completely gone to pieces, poor thing, and they have three kids under ten, so I've moved in with them for now."

"But you made the appointment and came along?"

She grinned at me. "Just checking you out to see if you can help Nicky."

"Yes. She has an appointment tomorrow, and I'll be happy for you to sit in."

Nicky, the victim's newly widowed wife, looked like she hadn't slept or eaten in a week. Gabrielle had to guide her into a chair. She sat, head hanging down, barely functioning.

Both of these reactions are frequent, as is a mixture of them, or experiencing each at different times. Some people mask the agony with efficient competence, being there for others, acting as if everything was all right. Others are completely devastated, in a state I can only describe as lostness. Neither of these reactions is better than the other. What is, is.

If the departed person suffered a lot of pain, or indignity as for example in dementia, there may be a sense of relief, even joy. My reaction to the phone call informing me of my mother's death was, "Thank heavens it's over." That was after six weeks of her being a frozen doll, with nothing moving except a still-active, still-brilliant mind.

The Impact period can sometimes last months, and as I said, it can return from time to time. The sufferer can think, "Am I going crazy?" Normality has been destroyed. The main reaction can be staying frenetically busy to hide from any emotion: being a sergeant-major to yourself so you have no time to think, and more important, no time to feel. For others, or for the same person at other times, it is helplessness: "I can't do this."

It is normal, even expected, to have what our culture considers to be hallucinations: hearing the dead person's voice, seeing flashes of the person. At the medically estimated time of Natalie's death, her brother and mother both felt hugged, with no physical person present to do the hugging.

In other, more discerning cultures, these are accepted as spiritual visits. A little story in *Lifting the Gloom* is fiction, but that can be truer than fact. Please read "<u>Eulogy for Paul</u>."

Even if you don't have such contact (or apparent contact), you will often engage in "as-if" actions: speaking of the person in the present tense, turning to say something to him, looking at the clock and wondering for an instant why she is late from work...

Loss of appetite, loss of interest in things in general, avoiding anything that threatens to be enjoyable, or the opposite, going overboard and desperately Having Fun can happen.

And the choice? The opposite of denial: acceptance: "Yes, it did happen."

This was almost immediate for Nicky, and because of this, she could progress with her grieving. Gabrielle's way of coping actually got in the way. Keeping her pain in a tightly sealed box took up a lot of energy. Three months after her son's death, she caught the flu, which developed into pneumonia. Only after her return from hospital was she able to acknowledge the reality of her loss.

Elizabeth Neeld titles her second choice **Stumbling in the Dark.** Yes, the loved person is gone, and the loss is acknowledged, but you are now in a living hell.

You're at serious risk when Stumbling in the Dark. You may court danger one way or another like driving unsafely, casual sex, substance abuse such as smoking for the first time in your life, walking alone in a dangerous neighborhood. For some people, this sinks to a definite, conscious wish to die. I will address suicide in a chapter of its own.

When I experienced serious grief years ago, I lost all motivation to do anything. Get up in the morning, go to bed at night. Nothing in between but dragging from moment to moment. There used to be plans and hopes and projects, but now, "What's the point anyway?" I went to work because I had a family to support and a mortgage to pay, and there I put a smile on my face. Actually, focusing on doing my job was a sort of a holiday from the hole in my life, but it was a false mask. The real me was an empty place inside a steel box with no light.

I emerged from this, but a few months later experienced an unrelated source of stress, and back I was into my steel box—until I climbed out again.

Similarly, the roles were reversed when Gabrielle came out of hospital. Nicky had to look after her. She'd been attending Nicky's sessions to be a support until her illness, but had declined further sessions for herself, until now. I visited her at home for session 2.

"What hurts," she said, "is being helpless. I am the one GIVING help, not GETTING help. And, well, this loss of, um, the kind of person I am has rubbed my face in... in... Tom's death." She started to cry.

I didn't make the mistake of telling her this was what she needed (one of the worst things you can do as a helper), but sat there, projecting caring and compassion without words until she stopped. Then I said, "You know all the things Nicky has tried that worked for her. What do you think will work for you?"

"Nothing will bring Tom back."

Stumbling in the dark. Note the combination of acceptance and devastation. This is not a "second stage," but as a second way of being. And whenever it occurs, it gives us the second choice. For some people, it's only once, for others over and over. But remember the power of NOW? (see p. 9)

At any moment while in this state, we have a choice. This is to look the situation in the face and decide to make whatever changes are necessary. And, as I said, we may have to do this more than once.

Many people need someone else to lead them out of the hell of "There is no meaning. I might as well be dead!"

I was paid to be that person for Gabrielle, but a trusted relative, friend or colleague is more frequent. Remember Margaret and Jim, who both felt responsible for the death of their toddler son, and also bitterly blamed each other? In her fourth session, Margaret came in looking strong and determined. She explained, "Met up with my older brother yesterday. He's visiting from interstate. He told me off for acting like a zombie and sat down with me and forced me to write out a list of what I need in the new life I have to build for myself."

That's Elizabeth's second choice.

And yes, you may need to design a new life for yourself several times, or to resume the new life you'd designed and then lost again.

Your physical health will probably worsen as a result of grieving, so the occasional medical checkup is essential. And yes, you deserve it, even if you have lost a loved one.

Elizabeth's third choice point is **Observation**, a title I found odd. The right choice is to realize that we attract into our life what we send out. We need to advance from "poor me." How does this happen?

Attention is a searchlight. Whatever it shines on stands out, with everything else retreating into background. When we are lost, we live in a world of darkness and suffering. Acquaintances, new and old, tell you their sad stories.

The choice is whether to shift attention or not. With Gabrielle, a standard cognitive-behavioral tool worked. I asked her to monitor several measures of her physical recovery and record this daily. This shift in attention in turn focused her on positives—and then more positives came into her life.

Brian was a high-rise construction worker in his fifties, who'd divorced some twenty years ago and moved back with his mother, who did everything domestic for him. When she suddenly died of a heart attack, his grief was absolute, made worse by helplessness: he didn't know how to cook, how to work a washing machine, or how to make a bed. Then of course there was the aching silence of loneliness. He was referred to me after a suicide attempt. In our fifth session he said, "OK, Bob, you're right. There is still a life to live, but how?"

"What will make life livable?"

He actually managed a grin. "Mother. Oh, OK, she ain't coming back. I would need to learn to do all the stuff she did for me, right? And hell, I need some friends."

"Have you ever heard of Men's Sheds?"

"Yeah, there's one not far from me. So, you reckon I should check it out?"

"Yes. And research books and courses that'll help you with becoming your own housemaid."

He did both. Having excellent practical skills, he soon became as much an instructor as member at the Men's Shed, which opened up a lot of positives.

And again, this is not a straight line but a yo-yo. Especially when at home, Brian regularly crashed, alone in a three-bedroom house. Then he had an idea: found a young woman and her two little children who were fleeing domestic violence, and invited them to share his house, rent free. This way, he acquired an honorary daughter and grandkids, and once again someone to look after his domestic needs. When we completed therapy a year later, there was no question of any romance between them, but they had settled into a comfortable long-term arrangement.

The fourth choice is **Turning Into the Wind**. This is the decision to turn from loss to living.

As I've said, grief is the emotional reaction to any kind of loss. Marjoram's loss was divorce rather than death, but her reaction was just as severe. Her husband had been verbally and emotionally abusive, and groomed her to believe that she was stupid, and helpless without him. Leaving her for a younger woman was the culmination of a long-term campaign of destruction, which had worked all too well.

Her prop became red wine, and she soon became addicted to alcohol. Only the needs of her young children kept her alive. Then, in another turn of the screw, the ex filed for custody of the children because as an alcoholic, she couldn't be trusted with them.

Her response was to park the kids with her mother for two weeks while she went into a residential rehab program. Thereafter, she attended Alcoholics Anonymous twice a week. Her mentor there was one of my ex-clients who referred her to me.

She got her lawyer to call me as an expert witness, and in court I delighted in laying out the systematic torture the man had subjected Marjoram to, and together with the Alcoholics Anonymous (AA) mentor, we were able to reassure the judge that she had her addiction under control.

This first-ever success against the man opened her eyes to a new insight: "I do a lot more than survive without the bastard. However it hurts, I can build a life for myself—and without the crutch of a brain poison."

This is the choice point of Turning Into the Wind: moving into a new life beyond the loss.

Remember, getting to this point is not automatic or foreordained. It needs work. There needs to be an explicit decision to move through the loss into a new life.

Once you've got there, you enter the next field of battle: **Reconstruction**. This one is about regaining meaning: What is life about? What should I strive for?

As the title suggests, this is when you put into action the plans for building a new life. It is action rather than merely plans and hopes. Brian, who'd lost his mother, managed it by finding a younger permanent replacement. This was the major achievement of building a good future.

This state is like the ebb and flow of a tide of strength. If things go well, we gradually climb, but always backward and forward. Marjoram kept struggling with alcohol, but after each slip she determinedly put the AA teachings into practice. When we parted company, she'd been dry for six months.

Many people enter Reconstruction, but find it way too hard. Then, any little setback feels like a major failure, and we can go right back to the agony of the initial loss.

Not all of my cases were successes. Sheree was the survivor of childhood sexual abuse, and also physical abuse you could see on her battered face. The two supports of her life were her older sister, and the minister of a local church. She was referred to me for grief counseling after the sister died of cancer. She seemed to be doing remarkably well, something I attributed to her religion. In her last session, on a Friday, she reported that she'd enrolled in a short course on developing photographs (that's how long ago this was, before the digital revolution), and seemed optimistic about getting a job and earning a living.

Sunday morning, I found a message on my phone, asking me to come to her place at 10 a.m. When I got there, the minister was also waiting, due to a similar invitation. After half an hour of not getting a response to knocks and phone calls, we called an ambulance. The paramedic kicked the door down, and we found her dead. She'd taken a bottle of sleeping pills dissolved in alcohol.

I don't know the reason for the setback, but probably what would normally be something minor (maybe thoughts like *I haven't studied in years. I'll probably fail* or perhaps *I don't know if I can face up to meeting new people!*) she crashed right back into devastation and couldn't cope with life.

This is despite having made the appropriate choice for Reconstruction.

Next, with luck, we **Find Solid Ground**. Elizabeth Neeld chose to do this by resigning from a secure job to work as a self-employed writer, and to realize that the dead person lives on in our hearts and is influencing us for the better in the present moment.

A forty-eight-year-old client of mine was diagnosed with a pituitary tumor. It so happened that her father had died on the operating table at forty-eight years of age, and she was convinced this was a family doom. My work with her was partly to deal with the horrid effects of this fear, partly on the unresolved grief for her father.

She had her operation, and it was successful, although it left her with a number of physical disabilities. The major change this led to: she started up a support group for survivors of pituitary operations, and those needing them.

Another client, who has stayed on as a friend, is Dennis. When he was seven years old and his brother five, their father murdered their mother in a drunken rage. But when Dad had served his jail term, he came out a changed man: a teetotaler, gentle, kind, thoroughly decent. Now a young adult, Dennis formed a loving bond with him, but Dad had died six months before Dennis was referred to me.

How did I know he had reached Solid Ground? He told me of a teenager whose family had just been destroyed by domestic violence, and whom Dennis had taken into his home. There was no formal adoption or anything like that, but this good man had acquired a child and a young buddy, and the kid had a role model to follow.

This is typical of the growth that can take place during Solid Ground.

Finally, there is **Daylight**. Elizabeth said she'd realized that she was done with grieving four years after her husband's death. Remember the woman who'd told Rose that after three months, she was surely over it?

The choice is to accept death as a part of life. It is. We can now experience joy, and have reached the goal I'd outlined on page 4. We have become stronger, like the healed fracture of a bone, more compassionate and empathetic—if we have made the right choices.

Part III:
The Two Parts of Grieving

Grief has two components: your loss, and compassion for the suffering of the dead person. This is the case even in situations where you are glad of the departure of an abuser. If you don't believe me, read on. Well, read on even if you do believe me.

Loss

Suppose that an interstellar ship is invented. Your daughter is accepted as one of the crew. This just has to be a cause of great pride, but... but you will never see her again. There can be no meaningful communication: once the ship has gone out of our solar system, messages will have a return time measured in years. You cannot ensure her safety, meet your grandchildren if any, be there to celebrate her joys and support her in her sorrows.

She is not dead, no, but she has left a huge hole in your life.

Your feelings of loss are exactly as for grief. This is a legitimate pain. It is the same kind of reaction as to losses that do not involve death, such as being fired from a job, or failing an examination and so missing out on the career you hoped for—only of course far more devastating. Later, I will offer you tools for easing it, and point you toward a path that leads you to eventual calm acceptance. For now, again, we need some first aid. When we collapse emotionally, we let go of precisely the things that make us strong. So, here are the **seven magic bullets** that will enable you to cope better with anything, even your terrible loss.

These are:

- Healthy, nourishing diet; not too much or too little.
- Adequate sleep; not too much or too little.
- Enjoyable exercise.
- Fun—yes, it is possible. People like first responders, firefighters, nurses keep going through humor.
- Creativity.
- Social connectedness.
- Meaning.

If you can manage to return these features into your life, you will do better at coping with anything. I originally researched this list for my book, *From Depression to Contentment: A self-therapy guide*, but it also helps with anxiety, overcoming addictions, burnout in your occupation, and yes, grief. You can read the relevant chapter at http://bobswriting.com/psych/firstaid.html.

As I said, the wording there applies to depression, and grief is not depression. But if you schedule your grief to specific times as I have recommended, then you can and should live the rest of your day as if life was normal. Any time a thought of grief comes, lovingly send it away to the appointed time.

So, please read what I have there, then continue.

The Seven Magic Bullets Adapted to Recovering From a Loss

Three of them—nourishment, sleep and exercise—apply in exactly the same way as in the online First Aid chapter. Here are the others.

Fun

It takes a great deal of effort to stay sad while you are laughing, or even smiling.

I use it all the time. You will notice a steady sprinkle of little jokes throughout this book on grieving. When all else fails, I find some way of giving myself a laugh, otherwise I'd feel a need to jump off the planet.

Fun is highly individual. What gave you enjoyment before your tragedy? Do your best to put it back into your life.

Many people react to this suggestion by feeling that enjoying themselves is disrespectful of the loss, but that's what scheduling is for. We are honoring the grief—during the appointed time. The rest of our day is intended to be as close as possible to what used to be normal.

Remember Margaret and Jim, whose marriage was wrecked because each blamed the other for the death of their toddler son? During their third joint session with me, I asked what used to give them enjoyment.

Jim said, "Dancing. That's how we met, during ballroom dancing contests."

"Yes, we originally had different partners, but when I danced with Jim, I realized we fit together so well... Until... until Kenny came along, we danced every Saturday evening." Margaret's eyes were awash with tears at the thought of her little son.

Jim grimaced in an odd way: a smile to hide the need to cry too. "We won a heap of medals, too."

I managed not to hug them. You are not supposed to do that to your clients. "Tomorrow is Saturday. Why don't you go dancing?"

Both looked dubious. Jim said, "I still want to bash my head into a wall or something. You can't, um, I dunno..."

"You can't have fun?"

"Yeah. Kenny is... is out of our lives, and, and..."

"And you can have fun. Give it a go."

Jim phoned me Monday morning, 9 o'clock. "Bob, I am calling to cancel the next session. We feel we don't need it anymore."

"Did you go dancing?"

Margaret said, "God bless you, Bob, we did, and um... returned to being husband and wife again."

Obviously, they had their phone on speaker. Jim took over. "Look, we got all your lessons in the head. I've taken notes after every session. I know we need to do a lot of work yet, but we'll be supporting each other."

I contacted them again for six-month follow-up. Jim said, "We're both still grieving for Kenny, have a meeting with him together for an hour every Sunday morning. And I've twisted Margaret's arm to return to study. You know that before we met, she was studying for further qualifications as a Maternal and Child Health Services nurse but stopped a couple months before Kenny was born. She's back in the course."

He said his baby's name without any sign of distress.

So you see, fun is not only possible while you are grieving: it can speed up the process in a way that continues to honor your loss.

* * *

One of my favorite books is *The Rugmaker of Mazar-e-Sharif* by Najaf Mazari. He is a Hazara: the ethnic group the majority Pushtun people of Afghanistan hate. Hazara have suffered genocidal attacks in the past and are constantly targeted by the Taliban.

Think of it this way. Losing one beloved person is terrible. A Jew in Hitler's Germany, a Rohingya in Myanmar, a Hazara in Afghanistan, or a Palestinian in the Gaza Strip experiences multiple griefs all the time.

Najaf ended up on a boat that sank in the Coral Sea. The Australian Coast Guard fished him and his companions out—then he spent years in a concentration camp, expecting every day to be deported back to torture and death.

He is one of the lucky ones and now owns an upmarket carpet business.

All the profits from his writing are used to benefit people back home in Afghanistan. This used to be girls' schools, but I suspect now it is helping people escape from the newly resurgent Taliban.

What brought this book to my mind? It is full of laughter. Najaf gently laughs at himself all through the report of his experiences and gets the reader to laugh with him.

If he can, you can. Do read the book.

Creativity

Here is a poem by my friend, Lauren Persons, which she wrote on the one-year anniversary of her husband's death. She has given me permission to reprint it here.

Mourning Coffee, by Lauren Persons

Mourning came this evening,
Barefoot and quiet.
Unlike her first appearance
When she defiantly refused a dress of tasteful black
And strode in a white, too-tight suit,
Her matching spiked heels digging into tile floors.

Mourning came this evening
In Halloween disguise,
Not ghoulish or foreboding
But in gauzy robes of memories
And masks of painted smiles.

Mourning came this evening,
and is known to come at dawn,
swishing in fuzzy slippers and
a pale blue wraparound robe,
pulled tightly at the waist.

And each time when she leaves,
I vow to be a better host.
And perhaps with every visit,
I will learn to be polite—
Serving endless cups of coffee
To every teaspoon, full of tears.

My mother died in 2000, and I wrote a book about her life. *Anikó: The stranger who loved me* is the hardest book I have ever written—and the one that won the most awards. It is written from the heart. Writing that book put my creativity to use in processing my grief. It is available in paperback and eBook formats wherever books are sold.

William Funchess suffered terribly as a prisoner of war in Korea. Years later, he wrote a highly successful book, published in 1999. "I got yellow pads and ball point pens and spiral notebooks and just started writing. The minute I finished writing, the nightmares stopped."

It is not necessarily creative to engage in activities such as painting, sculpting, writing, textile crafts, gardening, cooking, composing and playing music. They can be done in a routine, hack fashion. Rather, when something is done with full involvement, it is a creative activity regardless of what the activity is. Here is a little story, reproduced from my book, *Lifting the Gloom: Antidepressant* writings, available in paperback and eBook from bookstores around the globe.

Housework, in 200 words

One of my joys is to wash the dishes. The house came with a mechanical dishwasher, but I've never used it. You see, a biological dishwasher allows me to warm my hands in sudsy water on a cold day and softens the calluses from the physical work I do all day in our home renovation business.

What? Girls can't do that? Get a life! This one can!

Myra is a great cook. When she comes home, she creates magical meals with joy, so I clean up. Start with a mess +++, and end up with everything gleaming and tidy.

On Sunday morning, we clean the house together and make it a sort of a dance.

I toss stuff into the washing machine and hang it on the line. Just think how modern it is: a solar and wind powered clothes dryer! And when the weather won't allow that, there is always the clothes horse. Myra does the ironing, because for her it's a meditation. She always emerges from it with a new poem.

Housework is a process of creating welcoming beauty out of dirty chaos. Why on earth would we not enjoy it?

Have you noticed a pattern? Actually, creativity is enjoying an activity, done mindfully. Doing something creative is a holiday from suffering, builds your inner strength, and makes life worthwhile.

Starting with Viktor Frankl's *Man's Search for Meaning*, there has been a lot of research on what enables some exceptional people to survive, and to keep their inner dignity, in circumstances that devastate everyone else. Among these champion survivors are musicians, poets, artists.

One of them calls himself "Eaten Fish" because he nearly drowned during his attempt to seek asylum in Australia. He is from Iran, with many skills, including the drawing of brilliant cartoons. This has two benefits. Facing outward, he can be an effective social activist and communicator. Facing inward, his creativity protects his sanity. Learn more about him at https://eatenfish.com/.

Everyone can do things creatively, in any situation. You can, in yours.

Social connectedness

Almost everyone suffering from serious grief goes through a period during which they withdraw into a deep, dark hole and pull it after themselves. I know, for I've been there. Some never emerge, and this is one of the reasons for being "stuck in grief:" when the pain of the loss is never resolved.

Since you have started reading this book, you will never be alone again. I insist on being with you from now on, even if we never meet, even if I die tomorrow. I know that's possible, because I have the honor of supporting a great many people I have never met. For example, a nice young man in Sweden has my depression book on his phone. When he feels himself sliding into gloom, he reads a relevant chapter. A teenage boy somewhere in the USA contacted me because he was suicidal due to guilt over having sexually played with a couple of little kids when he was twelve years old. He is now self-accepting, and strong enough to teach the tools he has learned from me to people around him. He contacts me every month or so. This may be because he has backslid a little and wants me to hold his hand, or the opposite: he wants to genuinely check on me to see how I am doing.

And in January, 2022, I got this email:

> Hello Grandfather Bob,
>
> I hope this email finds you well. My name is Elle and I had emailed with you sometime back in 2019. I was struggling with intrusive thoughts and false memories. I'm now at a much more peaceful place. Not sure if you even remember me. But I had to reach out to let you know how appreciated you are.
>
> For a couple of weeks now I have felt compelled to email you, so I began to locate your webpage. Glad I found it. I want to thank you so much for taking the time to message me and care about me. You didn't have to do that, but you did. Today as I think back, it touches my heart and brings tears to my eyes to know beautiful souls like yours exist on this earth.
>
> I send all my love and good wishes to you.
> Sincerely, Elle

So, I will be delighted if I can hold your hand as well. You are welcome to send me a private message through the <u>Contact page of my blog, "Bobbing Around."</u>

The greatest resource for coping with grief is support from people who care. They don't need to do anything, say anything. You can unburden yourself to them or simply be silent in their company. It is connection at the heart that counts, which can even be at a distance. Knowing that someone a thousand miles away sends you love will help you to keep going.

All the same, personal contact is better. You may have distanced yourself from family and friends, and perhaps they reacted with hurt, and now there seems to be a permanent chasm.

I have seen this pattern with many grieving clients. For example, Sven was referred to me for depression, but during the first session I found out that five years previously, his only child had died at fourteen years of age, when he'd stolen a car and crashed it. Sven and his wife divorced three years later, and he had cut himself off from his family. He was a long-distance truck driver, and switched jobs a couple of times a year when colleagues started getting friendly. I asked him why.

"Look mate, I am only here because my doctor gave me a choice: antidepressants or therapy, and I can't do the drugs with my job. But actually, talking to you is helping. OK, everyone else has family. Wife, kids, a life to live. Me? Nothing. So, I hear them talking about it and envy eats me up. Rather than take it out on other people, I move on."

I gently said, "That's fair enough, much better than hurting others. But tell me, what would stop you feeling envious?"

After a long silence, he murmured, so softly that I'd have missed it if I hadn't seen his lips move, "If I had a family myself."

What about the family of your birth?

Another silence, while I beamed caring at him. "Yeah. Parents still alive, and I got a brother and a sister, but haven't seen any of them since Peggy got rid of me. They used to leave me phone messages, and letters through the mail and that, but stopped years ago."

"Because you never answered?"

"That's it."

"Why not?"

"What the f— would I say? I put food in one end and shit it out the other, get up and go to bed, drive the truck from here to there and back again... How exciting is that? I got nothing to say, so I don't say it."

"You're my mob," I told him. "For some people, conversation is lubrication. For us, it's information. I am no good at chatting either. Only, they weren't trying to contact you to find out anything but to offer something."

"What?"

"Love, caring, support. And I have a theory." This time, I paused.

"You going to tell me?"

"You know the story of the prodigal son?"

"I'm not religious."

"You can grab wisdom from any source." I summarized the story of "The Lost Son" for him (Luke 15:11-32), then, "So, write them a letter and see what happens."

"I still don't know what the f— to say."

"Sven, it's not about facts, but about feelings. Explain why you cut them off, and apologize, and ask for their support." Looking at his face, "I know. Big boys don't cry, and you don't whinge to anybody. But look. Our hour is nearly over. Write a letter, and we can spend our next session on making it perfect."

My estimate of the chances of him returning was 50-50. But he did, and sent a heartfelt apology, and this was the start of his recovery.

Here is another thing. It's almost a cliché: a recently bereaved person is walking down the street, and people cross the road to avoid a conversation. Why? "I don't know what to say..." This is unintended cruelty. At this time, the person needs social contact, not shunning. Much better is, "Hi Sue. I've heard about your tragedy. I don't know what to say, but I am here for you."

This may lead to tears, but they will be good tears; a small step toward healing.

I've already mentioned my little story, "<u>A Different Christmas Tale</u>" when discussing how to cope with special days like Christmas and anniversaries, but it is also a powerful illustration of how even one caring connection can make an enormous difference. All the same, research shows that for long term wellbeing, you need to be part of at least three circles. However, this can include loving connection to a pet, and the circles can overlap.

Your situation may be difficult, but I can guarantee, there are others as bad off, or even worse. Whatever the searchlight of your attention shines on stands out, other things are in shadow. So, shine it on how you can provide support for others who need it as badly as you.

At one stage, I was working with homeless people through a religious charity. Most of my clients were women fleeing domestic violence. When I put this suggestion to Vivienne, she told me the next week, "As you know, Bob, I've been getting some food by dumpster-diving at the local supermarket. After our session I went in and got brave enough to talk to the manager about them donating that throwaway food to Link (the charity funding her sessions). And he phoned the Link office, and it's all set up, ready to start next week, and I am now on the team!"

So, if you can find some way of being of benefit to others, you will gain social connections that will be of even more benefit to you. The more you give, the more you get.

Meaning

Way back when I was a research scientist, Alan and Beth were my mentors. They did everything together, and when cancer took Beth, Alan said, "All the chapters are written. I just want to close the book and be with her." He stopped caring for himself, stopped all his usual activities. His body listened, and he was also diagnosed with cancer. He refused treatment, and soon died.

And yet, he was younger than I am now, with a lot of wisdom. What he had lost was meaning.

So, when my stepfather died in 1999, I knew my mother was highly likely to follow him. To give her something to occupy her mind, I asked her to provide me with material so I could write her biography. I sent her a little cassette recorder. Over a year, she spoke onto a boxful of tapes, and filled several exercise books with handwritten notes, despite arthritis that made writing painful. She assembled a whole heap of documents and photographs. They were also helpful because they reminded her of her many achievements, and of the strength, courage, intelligence and determination that had made them possible. That reminiscence and research kept her alive and functioning, and using the fruit of her work helped me with my grief.

* * *

Ben saw me as a bushfire survivor, and he also told me of his father's transformation. For all of Ben's life, Dad had been the perfectionist, the savage critic, "My way or the highway," no praise but harsh discipline. Perfection was the meaning of Dad's life, and perfection is never possible, so Dad was never happy, and made sure no one around him was either.

At 70 years of age, Dad suffered a cardiac arrest and nearly died. He came out of hospital after his triple bypass operation a changed person. He called the family together including three estranged children and gave them all a heartfelt apology. While on what could very well have been his deathbed, he had a "<u>near-death experience.</u>" He learned what was important, and it was not things but people, not perfection but love. He felt immense regret for all the hurt he had imposed over the years, and for the rest of his life, his aim was, "When I do die, I want you all to remember me with love, not with relief that I am gone."

He'd changed the meaning, and that changed everything.

A final illustration of the power of meaning comes from Viktor Frankl. A terribly grieving widower came to him for counseling. After an hour's conversation, Viktor summed it up: "Your life is filled with sorrow because she is gone, and you're here."

"Yes."

"My friend, if you had died, and she survived, would she feel this terrible sorrow?"

"She would."

"Have you then not spared her this suffering?"

The Ceremony of Moving On

As I have shown, most people process grief, if slowly, with effort and frequent backsliding. But it is not a race: your pace of coping with your loss is exactly right for you. Eventually, though, you will hopefully reach the goal I set out on page 4.

I have a friend who was devastated when his life partner died. On the one-year anniversary of her passing, he called all his friends together and ceremonially planted a tree in a beautiful spot. He had a silver plaque made, which he attached to a large stone, marking this memorial for perpetuity. He led us in a prayer, then said, "I am single again."

This kind of ceremonial closure is very healing, but it does NOT need to be one year after the event. Rather, do it when you know you are ready.

Returning Life into Your Life

Let us recap.

Grief takes time, because its progression is hard work that takes time. However, that should not be all the time. That's what Rose's wonderful invention, scheduling, is for. By concentrating the bad, you can live the rest of your life as if it was normal.

This means using the seven magic bullets: eat well, ensure your sleep is restful, enjoy exercise, have fun, do things creatively, accept and give support, and reintroduce purpose and meaning. That last one is the hardest, but the most worthwhile.

During all this, work toward being able to live mindfully, in the Now. When you achieve it, even for brief periods, you are free of suffering.

And when you are ready, celebrate the end of your period of grieving with a special ceremony.

Compassion for the Departed

For several years as a teenager, I worked at a movie theater. We had to wear a bright red jacket and sell sweets and things to patrons before the show and during the intermission. This meant I watched each movie six times, except for the first five minutes and the last five minutes. Most of these shows were immensely forgettable, but a scene from a western came to me when thinking about the second part of grieving: concern for the departed. Our hero is trying to talk with a Mexican old woman, but they don't share a language. Through mime, she has managed to explain that her husband has died. To show he understands, he points toward heaven, with a questioning look on his face. She shakes her head, tears pouring down her face, and points down toward hell.

I am fortunate in that I don't believe in hell. This is a tricky point: I have neither the right nor the intention of arguing with people about their religion. If you follow a version of Christianity or

Islam that includes a belief in hell, that is your right, and it is proper for your emotions and actions to be ruled by that belief.

If this applies to you, please read the following sections anyway. We can respect each other's beliefs while I state mine and the evidence they are based on. You can disagree but still find nuggets of solace and comfort alongside the parts you reject.

That Last Sight

Transitions are usually painful. This applies to birth, and in many cases to death. If you were forced to witness the painful passing of a loved one, or are required to see the body, how can you not have your heart fill with compassionate sorrow?

In her first session, Rebecca's red, bloodshot eyes attracted my attention. So, my first question to her was if she had sleeping problems.

"I don't dare to go to sleep," she replied. "For the past three weeks, I've had the same nightmare every time I do."

"Are you willing to tell me what it is?"

To my surprise, she gave a big grin. "Why else would I be here? It's my mother on her last day in the hospital bed..." The grin was gone, horror twisting her face. "Tube up her nose, tubes into her arms, face like a skeleton, and every breath a rattle. Then she stopped breathing." She cried, hands covering her face.

All I could do was to send an imaginary beam of compassion at her. After a gap, I asked, "How long ago was that?"

"Oh, nearly a year. So, why did it start up now?"

"We can work on that later. Before that, I want to do first aid to get rid of the nightmares."

Distress gone, her face lit up. "Can we?"

"Do you have a photo of your mother at the best time in her life?"

"Yeah, I have her photo from her fiftieth birthday framed on the wall in our living room."

"OK, Rebecca, close your eyes and imagine that picture. Can you see it?"

"Yes."

As I am ethically required to, I explained hypnosis to her. "The process is, I get you very relaxed, then we go through a pleasant imaginary journey to a safe place of your choice. There, we'll work on your memory of your mother. The thing is, you'll be doing it all. If a suggestion of mine agrees with you, follow it. If not, you can modify it for yourself, or replace it, and it'll still work."

So, I talked her into a beautiful hypnotic trance, then asked her to see that picture of her mother. In her imagination, we enlarged the picture to full size, then had it come to life. Rebecca was BACK at her mother's fiftieth birthday.

Then I told her, "From now on, awake or asleep, whatever you're doing, wherever you are, this is the mother you'll remember."

She nodded, so slightly I'd have missed it if I hadn't watched for a sign of agreement.

Then, as is necessary, I gradually talked her back to normal consciousness.

And yes, this fixed the nightmare problem.

You may be free of nightmares but still have your memory of your lost one blighted by those last moments. Hypnosis is not necessary for replacing the distressing memory with a good one. Often, simply deciding to remember the person at a particular time is sufficient.

This will remove one frequent component of grief. It was also a necessary part of Margaret and Jim's healing. In an early session for each, we replaced the guilt-and-horror-ridden final memory with a happy moment in little Kenny's short life.

If Your God Is Loving

All the great religions share a common message, one that speaks to all of us, clothed in the culture of their origins. You can be an atheist and benefit from taking this message into your heart, and do your best to live by it.

In Christianity, this message is best stated in St. Paul's letter to the Corinthians:

> Love is patient, love is kind. It does not envy, it does not boast, it is not proud. It does not dishonor others, it is not

self-seeking, it is not easily angered, it keeps no record of wrongs. Love does not delight in evil but rejoices with the truth. It always protects, always trusts, always hopes, always perseveres.

You will find it in the Qur'an:

Do not be people without minds of your own, saying that if others treat you well you will treat them well, and that if they do wrong you will do wrong to them. Instead, accustom yourselves to do good if people do good and not to do wrong even if they do evil.

The legacy of Confucius is not a religion, but carries the same message:

Those who cannot forgive others break the bridge over which they themselves must pass.
Do not impose on others what you yourself do not desire.
Love others as you'd love yourself, judge others as you'd judge yourself, cherish others as you'd cherish yourself. When you wish for others as you wish for yourself and when you protect others as you'd protect yourself, that's when you can say it's true love.

Christians tend not to realize that this is also the essence of Judaism. Rabbi Hillel said, "That which is hateful to you, do not do to your neighbor. On this hangs the whole Torah; the rest is commentary."

Every other great philosophy I have studied states this, in different words. You will find an interesting collection at http://bobswriting.com/bill/metta.html

Unconditional love is not compatible with a hell. The very concepts of reward and punishment imply CONDITIONAL love.

I have a dear friend who is a minister of religion. One day, she had a son. The next day, he was dead. He was at the prime of his life, a respected scientist, a Scout leader and sports coach who did a lot of good wherever he went. I saw teenage boys cry at his funeral.

He left behind a loving wife and two children, and even now, several years later, our local community misses him.

I don't know what his mother felt in the small hours of the night, what private agonies she may have experienced, but I do know that her healing was remarkably fast. She accepted her sad loss, and had the strength to support her husband, grandchildren, daughter-in-law, and all her son's many friends and admirers.

Given her belief system, she knows that whatever faults he had, whatever mistakes he'd made, God has forgiven him. I have no doubt she has found prayer to be a path to inner peace.

This is the solace of religion, when it is truly and deeply felt. Many years ago now, when I was undergoing my recruit training in the Australian Army, we had a visit from two Chaplains. They told us of research about the resilience and mental strength of survivors of the hellhole prisoner of war camps during the Korean War. One example was Father Emil Kapaun, who died, but until the last moment kept his dignity, and constantly advocated for his fellow prisoners who referred to him as their "guardian angel." The inspiring story is available at <u>War History Blog</u>.

The message of these instructors was, of course, "Believe like we do, believe like Father Kapaun did, and you can survive anything, even being tortured to death."

Well, yes, but as I felt forced to point out at the time, just because a belief may be useful in some circumstances doesn't make it true. I cannot make myself believe in order to achieve some end.

About 7% of the world's population are atheists. Perhaps three quarters of people claim to follow one of the major religions, and many others accept other noble belief systems. However, I would think most of these are "Sunday Christians" and their equivalents who lack the deep inner connection to their God that Father Kapaun and my friend benefited from.

But if you are one of those people with a personal connection to your God, use it to survive anything.

Father Kapaun never tried to force his religion on his comrades. My friend has never tried to convert me to Christianity. The actions of both of these admirable people illustrate what the Dalai Lama has said: "My religion is kindness."

So, you can also be there for others during their hard times and yet avoid proselytizing. Should people decide to follow you in your beliefs, fine. But they are the children of your God, whether they do or not.

The next question is, can we get a similar benefit without holding such a religious belief?

We can.

Cabrini Pak has studied the accounts of many resilient survivors of POW camps. Deep religious belief was one of the sources of inner strength, but not the only one. John McCain, who later became a Senator, survived torture as a POW in Vietnam because of a deep commitment to serving his country. William Funchess, the man who told Father Kapaun's story, was determined to return to his wife.

Margit was born in Estonia, but her mother took her out of the country immediately at the end of the Second World war in order to escape the Soviet Union's clutches. She was referred to me for severe anxiety issues (Margit, not her mother) forty years later. She also told me of her father's incredible story.

He was conscripted into the Estonian army a few weeks after Margit's birth. His most valued possession was a small (black and white) photograph of his wife and baby daughter. He was captured, and spent years in a POW camp at the very eastern edge of Siberia. At war's end, all the prisoners of war were turned loose, without resources. Incredibly, he walked all the thousands of miles home, through hostile country, part of it through winter. What kept him going? You've guessed it: that little picture of love.

When he finally arrived home, his wife and daughter were long gone, but an international agency eventually reunited them.

My conclusion is that living for something larger than ourselves, being of service to a deity, a person, a group, or even an individual gives us inner strength that speeds healing after tragedy.

Again, that's all very well. If you have such a commitment, it will serve you, but you cannot choose to devote your life to someone or something in order to gain that strength. But doesn't this go back to meaning, the seventh magic bullet?

You may benefit from returning to my article "<u>First Aid for All Sources of Suffering</u>" and re-read what I wrote to the teenager I named Crissie. She explicitly rejected religion, and yet my words led her to the same kind of solace by presenting the message of all the religions in secular terms.

Part IV:
Coping Techniques

Your Body is a Spacesuit for Surviving on this Planet

This is a quote from my friend and teacher (although we have never met), Petrea King. When she was thirty-two years old, an insensitive doctor told her, "You won't see next Christmas." As I write, she is now eighty and still going strong. After her recovery, her life's work has been supporting people with often fatal diseases like AIDS, cancer, muscular dystrophy, and multiple sclerosis. Her Quest for Life Foundation has helped tens of thousands of people live better, and as we all must sometime, to die well, with peace in their hearts.

What did Petrea mean by saying, "Your Body is a Spacesuit for Surviving on this Planet?"

Think about the implications. I am not a body, a mechanism of meat and bone and nerves and hormones, but a passenger in such a thing, for now. I find this immensely comforting. If this is true, then death is not the end of a book, but only the end of a chapter. It is only a temporary parting from loved ones who have passed over; that broken bone I mentioned at the start, not an amputation.

Knowing that we have lived before birth and continue after death is incredibly reassuring. Yes, our loved one has gone to another place, for now, but when we have fulfilled our tasks in this life, we'll meet again.

All through the nineteen months of anticipatory grief for Natalie, I felt immense compassion and helplessness because I couldn't help, couldn't ease her suffering. I kept hoping for a miracle like what turned Petrea's cancer off. But my belief in what happens after death eliminates the second half of grieving: "If she dies before me, I will grieve for the hole she has left in my life, but not for her."

However, as I said on page 39, just because a belief has good consequences doesn't make it true. Humans are champions at wishful thinking. As a scientist by training, I don't believe anything but go with the evidence.

Many millions of people know that they have lived before being born because they have experiences that can only be interpreted as past-life recalls. I am one of them, as you can read in my fictionalized autobiography, *Ascending Spiral*. We include atheists, and followers of religions that explicitly reject reincarnation.

But also, there is remarkably good scientific evidence that reincarnation occurs. If you are currently in the grip of grief, I am sure the last thing you want to do is to wade through scientific stuff, so I've posted three essays to my blog. They are:

- <u>Past life recalls</u>
- <u>Yvonne Rowan's story</u>
- <u>The other side of death</u>

For now, here are my conclusions:

- If a case before a court of law depended on the evidence for life after death, the judge would rule to accept it.
- A Guide meets you with complete, nonjudgmental, unconditional love.
- You are led to reexperience the significant events of your life, so you can build on your strengths, choose restitution to pay for your mistakes, and choose the lessons you want to learn in the next life.
- Suicide, however, means that you need to return to a situation in which you need to face the very challenges that drove you to despair, so you have a chance to do better.

When I wrote *From Depression to Contentment*, I was only aware of one line of evidence, but since then I have found two others. In addition to past-life recalls, there are reports of "near-death experiences" (when someone revives after clinical death), and verified communications from dead people.

All three are situations in which someone makes a factual claim they cannot possibly know. In addition, some children can exercise a skill they cannot possibly have acquired, combined with such factual claims.

When you have the emotional capacity to do so, please read Yvonne's account of how she returned from death twice, and the two essays setting out the scientific evidence for life between lives. If this conflicts with your religion or personal philosophy, it is perfectly all right for you to decline to share my belief. It is a major tool for contentment for me, but there are many others.

I find reincarnation to be a wonderful solace, and a major source of consolation when grieving. Yes, the most important person in my infancy, "Aunt Janka," died in 1951. Yes, my mother died in 2000. Yes, my daughter, Natalie, died in 2024. What these three spirits have done is to get rid of bodies that no longer served them. They had learnt all the Lessons they could with the personalities they had formed and needed to progress to new Lessons.

Remember my metaphor about your daughter being chosen to be part of the crew for an interstellar ship? Death is not that at all. She has merely moved to a different continent. One day, you'll go there, too, and one day, she will return, although in a different body, with a different but still recognizable personality.

Here is a poem I wrote for the husband of a lady I cared for (in both senses of the word) when I was a nurse. She was a Wiccan, which is one of the noble religions, and includes belief in reincarnation:

To a Grieving Husband

She will return.
Having lived the joys and agonies,
ecstasies and sorrows of this life—
to do better the next time around.

Will her passing make you a better person,
as her presence did, by your side?
Her school is in recess for now,
for she has passed, though our examination is still to come.
She will return.
The memory will never fade, but the pain will ease.

I have already referred you to <u>Eulogy for Paul</u> to illustrate "hearing his voice," but it is also highly relevant here.

So, while the hole in your life is real and terribly painful, you need not sorrow for the departed one.

* * *

Some thirty years ago, our friend, Annette, developed cancer. Her husband, Hans, cared for her with love, and until she died, his every waking moment was devoted to her welfare.

At the funeral, Hans played his guitar and sang a merry song. When he saw everyone look shocked, he explained, "This is her favorite song. She is with us right now and can hear it. I'm playing it for her."

His love for her was genuine. All the same, he showed no signs of grief, then or later, and after a year, married another lady.

What protected him from the pain? He was sure, deep within his heart, that she was, and is, fine. She had been released from an all-too-painful body and continued in a new form. I don't know how he protected himself from the pain of being without her, and unfortunately, we have lost contact so cannot ask him. But certainly, belief in reincarnation protected him from grief for his departed wife.

I wrote this long before Natalie developed cancer and died after 19 months of suffering. Now I find myself in the same situation as Hans. I am surrounded by constant reminders of her, since many of her possessions ended up in our home. And yet, apart from a few "if only" and "I wish" thoughts, I am not in pain. I know she is OK, so I am OK. I've done all the necessary grieving through her illness and have now "resolved my grief."

Infant Souls Don't Grieve

Hans didn't need to grieve on Annette's behalf because he was fully confident that she was still around, merely no longer attached to a painful body. At the other end of spiritual development are people who don't grieve because they lack empathy. It's like an emotional colorblindness. We call them psychopaths or sociopaths, but such labels are unhelpful.

"I hurt because you are suffering," or even "I hurt because you may be suffering" requires us to put ourselves in the other person's place, to intuitively know what it must be like in their situation. That's empathy. Empathy-blind people cannot do this. For them, other people are either tools or obstacles. If they lose a "tool" such as someone who provides them with money or does domestic work for them in combination with sexual services, then they simply replace that tool with another. It may be inconvenient, annoying— but not painful.

If you were an infant soul like that, you wouldn't be reading this book.

"The pain I feel now is the happiness I had before. That's the deal."
— C.S. Lewis
on the loss of Joy Davidman, his wife aged 45

Is it worth it? Would you like to be the kind of person who is unable to feel love for another?

Grieving Is Something You Do

It is all too easy to identify with our suffering. Before I learned mindfulness-based pain management, I dealt with physical pain by attempting to block it out, but this doesn't work for severe agony. In 1980, I had the bad judgment of tearing a cartilage within my knee. For hours, life was a pulsing scarlet hell that swallowed the whole world.

The same is true for emotional pain, except it lasts longer than an acute physical injury. But then, you probably know this already. The source of your pain may have been the death of an essential person in your life, or the impact of a disaster such as a flood or wildfire that has destroyed your home and your whole community, or the business that provided your livelihood going bankrupt. Regardless of the reason for your grief, it can feel like it has taken over your whole life. "I am the pain."

This is an illusion. I am not the pain, but the person experiencing it. And here is the path out: ask, with Jon Kabatt-Zinn, "Is my experience of pain in pain?" Humans are complex beasties, with many components to our consciousness. By identifying with the observer that notes the pain, we can distance ourselves from it.

One standard method is to rate it. Out of 10, how severe is your feeling of loss, right now? Even if it is 10/10, so bad that life isn't worth living for this moment, by rating it you have moved away from having it swallow you.

I am merely embodied in that painful body. I am the person calmly rating that horribly unpleasant sensation. I am merely the experiencer who experiences my loss. I am not that loss, but the person who is calmly rating how severe it is at this moment.

My reaction to the unfortunate event is justified. It is OK to feel it, to accept it, to live with it, for now. I can be content with my life, even if its content includes a painful body or a painful loss.

When I can do this, I can be fine in the middle of disaster. When I cannot do it for now, I can be fine with experiencing pain. After all, it is justified. And when I cannot be fine with accepting the experience, then I can be content, knowing that for now life is not worth living. Change is the only constant, so this, too, shall pass.

It does.

Wanting to go

Especially if the loss was unexpected, there is often a period of emotional numbing. Life becomes flat, as if you were a robot. Everything is drab, monochrome, meaningless.

This is a slippery slope, although most people climb out of it as the shock wears off, and life goes on.

I have already covered the tools for never going there, and how to climb out—but some people in this situation lack the motivation and energy to do anything. And unless something—or someone—interrupts the downward spiral, it's too easy to just want to die.

People caught in this trap won't be reading a book about grieving, or anything else. What they need is a caring friend. Usually, they lack the energy to say no to pretty well anything, but then are unable to cooperate. The best way you can offer help is to gently, lovingly pressure this person to see a psychologist or grief counselor. Then you may need to be the calendar and memory, and, still gently and lovingly, ensure the appointment is kept.

Often, having obligations for someone else's welfare can get a person through this period, and then be able to grieve. "Mother, I know it's unbearable, but I am suffering too. I need you." Such a plea may be the thing to start Mother on the way to recovery. Unfortunately, this is not always the case, and young children can be neglected, or a business allowed to slide into bankruptcy, because of grief.

If you have a friend or relation in this awful situation, you have the power of guiding them out of it. Gently, lovingly, persist in ensuring a reasonable diet, engaging in the acts of daily life, contact with others, and so on.

Here is an inside view of this state of (non)being, from *The Travels of First Horse*:

Horse withdrew into a place where nothing existed except his grief. The troupe traveled, and gave performances, but Horse took no part in this. He didn't even look after his horses. Miháj looked after him. He was the carer of animals and of hurt things, and Horse would have died without such care. Miháj said, "Eat this," and Horse pretended to eat, for it would have taken more energy to resist than to comply. Miháj commanded, "Have a wash," or "Go to bed," or "Get up and dress," and Horse did as he was told, because that was the easiest path. Gudrun was dead, and nothing else mattered.

People in this state have died from grief, or summoned sufficient energy to kill themselves. It takes a helper, in the story Miháj, to ensure survival.

You may succeed if you take on this noble task and start the sufferer on the road to recovery. You may fail, and the person may die through suicide, or like my friend Alan, by developing a rapidly fatal disease. It is absolutely essential for you to be prepared for this possibility, and know:

You Can Never Walk Another Person's Path.

It is NOT your failure if, despite your best efforts, this person dies anyway. All we can do is the best we can do, and the outcome is never in our control.

Later in the book I'll examine the purpose of life. For now, I'll simply state my conclusion: we are all apprentice Buddhas; apprentice Jesuses, or whoever your deity or ideal human is. Caring for the welfare of another person is exactly the kind of activity that leads to your spiritual growth. Success or failure is irrelevant.

Loss of Support

I met Nancy after she had attempted suicide. She was seventeen years old, overweight, with pimples on her forehead, and I noticed the scars of "cutting" on her wrists. I thought she was reacting to her appearance, as so many people do. In the first session, she revealed an abusive family, but it took until the third session for her to tell me the real reason for her distress. For the past eleven years, since they had moved to their current address, the anchor in her life was the old lady next door. Nancy visited her daily, did her homework there rather than in the chaotic and dangerous family home, and "Aunty Dot" was more family than the people genetically related to her.

And, three months ago, Aunty Dot had died. I am sure you guessed it. Why else would I remember this now? But at the time, it came to me as a surprise. Nancy's pain was severe and legitimate grief, and the suicide attempt was "to join the only person who ever loved me."

What helped her to decide to keep living? I gently asked her, "If Aunty Dot was sitting here with us, would she want you to do that, or to build a good life for yourself?

We did have seven more sessions after I posed this question to her, but her thinking about this issue was the turning point.

It's My Fault

Guilt is another reason for wanting to be dead.

Vlad was driving, with his wife beside him and their three children in the back, when he lost control on a gravel road and smashed into a tree. He survived with several injuries, but, sadly, the rest of the family died. I had my first session with him three weeks later, after his transfer to a hospital near where I live. His right leg was in elevated traction and tubes went into his body in various places. He told me, "All I want to do is to join them. Hell, if only I'd driven slower!"

"So, you feel as if it was all your fault?" The "as if" is reframing: I was subtly doing my best to introduce less certainty into his self-bashing. People don't tend to notice it but are influenced by it anyway.

Next step was what I have said in my first chapter: "Believe it or not, other people have been in your exact situation and have rebuilt their lives." Then it was helpful to simply make him feel heard and validated, accepted and even loved.

Since he had no other family locally, I visited him daily and sat with him for an hour, even though I was only paid for one session a week, and he knew this. I worked on my laptop computer unless and until he wanted to talk with me. Remember, social connectedness is one of the seven magic bullets. This unspoken connection helped more than anything. The message was, "I consider you to be worth spending my time to keep you alive," and this got him to feel that he was worth keeping alive.

By the time he was discharged from the hospital, we had an agreement that he would not kill himself, and I asked him to design how he would spend the rest of his life to make restitution for his mistake.

I am not some sort of a saint. Visiting him was a ten-minute detour on working days and an easy walk on days off. I was writing a book (as usual), and the secretary of several committees (as usual), and my psychotherapy practice also involved administrative tasks. So, for three weeks I did by his bedside what I'd have done at home. No big deal, right?

All the same, I saved a life. You can, too.

The Things Wrong with Suicide

My friend, T. A. Sullivan, is an acknowledged expert on auras, and has reported knowledge of the "other world" beyond death. She wrote:

> The largest consequence you face when transitioning from life after committing suicide is the fear and depression that you carry with you.
>
> Most suicides are people who are so frightened and so depressed that they can't find any valid reason to stay in the physical world. These emotions are carried with you and can color your transition. It may take you moments or eons to come to terms not only with the decision you made, but with the turmoil you created for yourself and those you left behind.
>
> There may be unfulfilled commitments and agreements (on a soul level) that you abandoned because of your suicide.

There are milestones within your own life that will be left unfulfilled, and your overall life's goals will be left incomplete.

How you deal with this incompletion will be up to you and any other souls involved. If they want to skip the whole thing and just continue with their lives as best they can, then no harm done. However, if they find that everything they wanted to do and accomplish is no longer possible and they have to change all their goals and lessons because of your actions, well... then you'll probably have to work with them again in another life to make good on all your abandoned promises and agreements.

These are just some of the reasons why suicide is considered one of the most selfish acts there is. Because the fear and depression keep you from recognizing just how deeply your actions can affect everyone else.

So, not only do you spend time trying to get over all the negative emotions you drag with you into the afterlife, but you'll also have to deal with all the other folks whose lives you disrupted.

<u>You can check her blog.</u>

Consequences

Someone asked the Dalai Lama, what was the greatest regret of his life. He said, an old monk once came to him, asking to study a particular Buddhist discipline. The Dalai Lama gently explained that this needed to be started at seven years of age. In his current life, the old man couldn't possibly do it. So, the man killed himself, presumably in the hope of being able to take the relevant path in the next life.

This cannot work. Suicide was such a debit on the man's karma that, after death, he was certain to require restitution for the act in the next life. Being denied the opportunity for learning this discipline is the only possible restitution.

The same goes for suicide for any reason, or no rational reason at all. It's a way of running away, probably from the very lesson situations the person was born for. As with the processing of trauma, running away from it only prolongs it. Suicide never works to solve problems, only to have them repeat.

The best way to deal with any problem is to face it and go through it. Grief is no different.

I Hated Him but Now I Miss Him

Our life has structure. A change in any part involves losses.

Greta originally came to me because of domestic violence. You could see it on her face: slightly crooked nose, a missing front tooth, and that defeated look of a victim. She had endured eighteen years of abuse, but her husband's grooming induced her to believe that she had nowhere to go.

And then he got into a drunken fight and died in the ambulance on the way to the hospital.

Financially, she and her teenage children were secure, except that she had no idea about accessing the bank accounts, budgeting and the like. Financial abuse is almost invariable in her situation. I referred her to a financial counsellor, who sorted out the immediate problems and educated her on relevant issues.

Six months down the track, she said to me, "At first, I felt joy—'the bastard's gone!'—but I... I feel guilty that I miss him."

"Let's examine this. Would you want him back?"

"No way!"

"Greta, close your eyes... A few deep breaths..." I'd taught her relaxation and meditation in our earliest sessions and now saw her relax. "Put yourself in a situation when you miss him. When you're ready, tell me about it."

After a silence, she softly, hesitantly said, "There's no one to tell me what to do... I need to make all the decisions... Yeah, the fear is gone, but, but, there is nothing in its place. I'm in a... an emotional vacuum, like."

I don't know if you are in this situation. If not, imagine it. How do we escape from an emotional vacuum?

Remember the seven magic bullets? They are a great start. In particular, I encouraged Greta to engage in creative activities, and to deliberately have fun. Then I moved to the most important magic bullet by asking, "What was the meaning of your life while Ron was still alive?"

"Survival." We'd worked this out months previously, but I needed it as the starting point of her new life.

"OK, Greta, what's my next question?"

Good. That got laughter. "What's the meaning of my life now, right?"

"Right. See, you don't need me, you can do it yourself."

She looked down, then out the window, then into my eyes. "Rebuilding."

She was on the way.

Hate and Forgiveness

Hate is a great motivator, but it is poisonous. The Buddha said, "Anger is a hot coal you pick up to throw at someone, but it's your hand that gets burned." Perhaps paradoxically, hate can get in the way of processing grief. This is true both for hating someone who has done you harm, and for self-hate.

Margaret and Jim suffered both. Here is what happened during Margaret's ninth individual session. Jim also achieved a similar set of insights at that time.

I started by saying, "My dear, you've come a long way. What's your biggest load left?"

She looked down, thinking, and I gave her time. "If only... If only he wasn't so quick and slapdash! If only I'd locked the screen door!"

I nodded. "Yes. 'If Only' is a terrible load. How'll we get rid of it?"

She managed a half-smile. "You're the expert!"

"I'm the expert on what's worked for me, and on the research evidence on what's worked for other people in your kind of situation. But you're the expert on Margaret."

"If... if I could let it go, somehow. But I don't think it's possible."

Bingo. She got it by herself, so now she owned the solution. Much better than me telling her. "It worked for me. Oh, my problem was nothing as terrible as yours, but it did give me a heap of suffering until I forgave my abusive stepfather. But tell me a little more about your attitude to Jim." Remember, this was after eight fruitful and sometimes stormy sessions.

"At first, all I wanted was a time machine to get him out of my life or banish him to Mars or something. Now... Yeah, I know he feels about himself the way I feel about myself. But forgive him? No way!"

"Margaret, forgiveness doesn't mean forgetting, or excusing, or allowing lack of responsibility. It means disapproving of the action, but giving unconditional love—not romantic love, but the same kind of love you might have for a tree or a deer or a grandmother. And what you said is actually an excellent first step: compassion."

"Oh." I saw the wheels turning. She had obviously never made the distinction between act and actor.

"Before... before our tragedy, I loved him. He has his faults, hell, so do I, so does everybody, but, yeah, he's a great guy. If we could undo this, I'd still be in love with him. So, um, as long as I can hold him responsible for his, what's the word? negligence, I forgive him as a person."

An invisible glow joined the two of us, and it wrapped around Jim, too, although he was not present. "Wonderful," I said. "If you don't watch it, you'll fool me into thinking I am a good therapist."

We shared a giggle, then I went on. "The next step is far more difficult. What will it take for you to forgive yourself?" This is a debating trick, because it assumes that it's possible.

She fell for it, after another thoughtful silence. "If... if Jim forgave me in the same way. He can take my opinion, then I can take his."

So, our next session was the first with both of them present. I'd written out a contract:

We, the undersigned, each forgive the other for the action that took all the light out of our lives, and accept each other's forgiveness with gratitude.

We will now cooperate in rebuilding our lives, even if separately. We promise to support each other in our recovery.

______________________________   dated ________
Margaret Jones

______________________________   dated ________
James Jones

______________________________   witness
Bob Rich

They signed two copies, one to be kept by each.

Forgiveness is the greatest healing force there is. I was terribly depressed during my childhood and youth, because of unrelenting abuse from my stepfather. Forgiving him was the first and largest step in my recovery in my 20s. In my 40s, the greatest step toward permanent healing and gaining maturity was forgiving myself for all the many ways I have hurt others. Part of my meditation routine is to say this beautiful Buddhist prayer, with specific events in mind:

If anyone has caused me harm, knowingly or unknowingly, accidentally or on purpose, I offer forgiveness.
If I have caused harm to any being, knowingly or unknowingly, accidentally or on purpose, I ask for forgiveness.

At my blog, you can read <u>two conjoined stories</u> from *Lifting the Gloom* with this theme.

Stuck in Grief

Sometimes, a person simply doesn't heal from grief. It goes on and on. Elizabeth Neeld's book *Seven Choices* starts with a story about a widow who cried at every reminder of her husband's death, and this was triggered by all sorts of things, such as chocolate for dessert. Only, the lady had carried this intense, acute grief for eighteen years!

In my work, I've found five reasons this may happen: putting the dead person on a pedestal; ongoing anger; social isolation; guilt; and masking the pain of grief with medication, alcohol or some other drug. Typically, more than one can be active, interacting in a very damaging way.

Mummified grief

Luigi is a lovely man. His joy is to be of benefit to other people, and the more they need him, the more he likes it. He and his wife migrated from Italy to Australia as a just-married couple. They had three sons—then she died. He was a wonderful single father while running a successful business as an electrician, and they grew into decent young men.

Then he met Kylie. Although she was twenty-one years his junior, they fell in love and married with his sons' blessing. They had a daughter... then five years later, Kylie developed lung cancer and died after another three years.

He was never my client. We met when I needed an electrician, and a friend recommended him.

When I phoned him, he said, "I don't do much sparkie work anymore but am in partnership with my sons owning five rental properties, and I look after them. But tell you what, next Saturday I'm taking my grandkids to the Sanctuary (a world-famous zoo for Australian native animals in my little town), and I'll call in afterward."

They arrived mid-afternoon: Luigi, short, muscular, smiling, his daughter, Alanna, a dark-haired beauty of eighteen, and three tired but happy little kids. Luigi fixed my problem in about an hour, then refused to accept payment. After some friendly argument, he did accept signed copies of three of my books.

But while he was working, and my wife entertained the grandkids with her home baking, Alanna took me aside. "My mother died ten years ago. Oh, it was terrible for a long time, but I've come to terms with it. But Dad... for him it's like it was yesterday."

"Has he had any counseling?"

"No. He sent me to a psychologist who helped a lot, but nothing and no one can talk him into accepting help. There is a room in our house that used to be her office, and nothing must be disturbed in there." She wrinkled up her nose. "The windowsill is covered with dead flies, and dust on everything, Mum would actually hate it. But it's a... what's the word? A mausoleum."

You cannot force healing onto someone who doesn't want to heal, but at least I could help Alanna. So, I gently asked, "Is he happy being in this state? Is it OK for him to feel as if she'd died yesterday?"

Luigi was happy to grieve for the rest of his life. However, you may be stuck in grief and hate it. "If only I could let go..."

You can, but it needs to be a deliberate, conscious decision, one of Elizabeth Neeld's Choices (if you can't remember which, you'd better do some revision). No one else can do this.

Remember the ceremony to signal the end of the period of grief (page 34)?

Ongoing Anger

One of my early clients perfectly illustrates how anger gets in the way of healing.

Briefly, a woman held onto anger aimed at the murderer of her younger brother. Using Narrative Therapy, I helped her to see herself and her situation in a way that got in the way of this anger, and this changed everything.

Isolation

I've already illustrated being stuck in grief because of social isolation. Remember the long-distance truck driver I'd called Sven? His son had died five years before. He didn't talk about it. Only the special atmosphere in a psychotherapy setting drew it out of him. This was why his doctor diagnosed him with depression instead of ongoing grief. He could work on the grief once he reconnected with his family. This included the boy's death, Sven's feelings of guilt (if only I'd been home more, he wouldn't have been the kind of kid who steals a car), and the breakup of his marriage. Once he could talk about these issues, he was able to progress with processing his grief.

When you serve by fighting in a war, other members of your unit often become dearer to you than family. Your life literally depends on their support, and both duty and emotion dictate that you risk your life for their safety and survival.

And some of them die, or are horribly handicapped for life, or break under the strain and become shadows of themselves.

Unfortunately, the culture of the warrior induces bottling up grief. You can feel alone and isolated because your comrades hide their grief, so you feel as if you alone were such a "weakling." And when you return to civilian life, you can be sure that few people appreciate or understand your pain.

This is the worst kind of social isolation, because it is invisible.

The same can be true for police, first responders, doctors and nurses, though at least for them the people they grieve for are usually strangers rather than the occupants of their heart.

I don't have to explain what the solution is. Find someone you can trust and bring your grief out into the open. A grief counselor or psychologist, a minister of religion, or a wise friend or relative are typical audiences.

There are support groups, including online. Find them and use them, and remember, the more you give the more you get. Be there for others in their grief and accept their compassion for yours.

Guilt

This is the worst load to carry. We've already seen its terrible effects on Jim and Margaret. The message is, "I did such a terrible thing that I deserve to suffer for the rest of my life."

If you have read with care, you'll know the cure for guilt: self-forgiveness, which is probably one of the most difficult achievements. Thank heaven, I have never been responsible for the death of another human being, but in my opinion, imposing suffering is even worse. And, because of my negligence, many years ago, a calf suffered a terrible injury. My conclusion was that I would need to reincarnate as an animal in a later life and suffer similar pain. But when I mentioned this to a wise friend, she asked, "What was the result of that experience on you?"

"I've gone out of my way to avoid harming any other living being."

"So, you have learned this lesson, and don't need to learn it again."

This little story was one of the new insights that helped to give a new meaning to Jim and Margaret's tragedy. After recounting this story, I asked each of them (one in the fifth session, the other in the sixth), "How has little Kenny's passing changed you for the better?"

Jim said, "I used to feel contempt for people who made bad mistakes, but hell, I can't do that anymore. Nothing anyone's done is as bad as my mistake. All my arrogance is gone, and I'm better for it."

Margaret's response was "I... um... I'll work for a world where all kids can live well and safely."

Vlad, the man whose family died when his car skidded out of control, applied to join the police after his physical recovery. While he didn't pass the very exacting fitness test, he got a position as a dispatcher: you know, the person who answers your emergency call. He also spent a lot of volunteer time giving talks on safe driving in high schools. Four years after he stopped therapy, he invited me to his wedding, to a teacher.

So, all three of these people grew spiritually, thanks to their feelings of guilt. Can you do the same?

Hiding Behind a Chemical Mask

Andrew was referred for severe depression three weeks after his father-in-law's death. He explained, "Bob, look, I can't sleep, can't eat, can't do my work. I'm tied into a knot. There are these thoughts and images going round and round in my head and, hell, it's hardly worth being alive!"

"I'll teach you a few tools for dealing with intrusive thoughts, whatever they are, but first, what are the thoughts about?"

"That's the crazy part. It's about my dad, not so much about my father-in-law, who was a good bloke and we were close, but... yeah, it's more about my own father."

"Hmm." (Yes, psychologists do say that.) "How long ago did he die?"

"A bit over five years."

I had a strong suspicion of what the problem was, and checked it out. "During those five years, did you just carry around the pain of his passing?"

He wriggled in his seat. "No. That's the odd thing. Life was fine until Robyn's dad died. I started crying inside about Dad during the funeral, a couple of weeks ago."

"How did you cope at the time, five years ago?"

"My doctor put me on Prozac, and then weaned me off it 18 months later."

There it was.

The antidepressant masked the symptoms and allowed Andrew to carry on without undue distress—but it stopped the grieving process.

Grieving is not a matter of the passage of time, but of going through certain activities, certain experiences. These are unique for each person, depending on past history, culture, inner resources— but they must take place for the grief to be resolved.

At least, Andrew's crutch was a drug that doesn't cause permanent harm. Using alcohol or other addictive drugs to drown out your sorrows is far worse, and, sadly, very common.

Think of it this way. Any traumatic experience, including the passing of a loved person, is like a journey. You get on a train at the death and arrive at the destination I set out at the start of the book. But if you get off the train, you'll never arrive. Never mind how uncomfortable the trip may be, you need to complete it. This means you need to feel the pain. There are no magical shortcuts.

Anticipatory Grief

There is no set path through grief. Everybody's experience is different. Rose, the inventor of scheduling, had cared for her husband through three years of cancer, and was completely devastated when he finally passed away. (p 6) All the same, by and large, people who do some of their grieving before death have an easier time of it after.

I have. I am now doing fine after my daughter's death, partly because I have already done my grieving. Oh, this morning we ate the first fruit from a young plum tree, and I had the thought, *Natalie will be interested when she phones tonight.* Then of course I realized, she is never going to phone again. I was sad, but not devastated the way the rest of my family is currently.

My mother-in-law was able to live independently until the very end because two of her daughters visited her daily and were a phone call away. They saw her health gradually deteriorate and handled emergencies. Her other relations saw her only on special occasions, when, like we all do, she put on a special show.

They found it a shock when she died, despite being told of her failing health. Some of her grandchildren got teary years after her passing, while, you've guessed it, the two carers came to terms with the end of her life relatively quickly and smoothly. It helped that they felt relief that she was liberated from a steady slide toward incontinence, unsteady walking, and difficulty breathing. The old lady retained her intelligence to the end, but this led to depression, and wanting to go. Knowing this, witnessing it first-hand, allowed acceptance.

I have seen this many times during decades of working in nursing homes: the regular visitors coped much better with a person's steady decline and eventual death than the Christmas flybys.

Two of my related clichés are "The more you give, the more you get," and "The more you give, the more you grow." If you love someone who is gradually sliding toward death, whether from old age or a chronic health condition, being their support benefits your loved one, and helps you, too.

Not all of us have the opportunity to do this, but whatever contact you can organize will help.

Reaching out

This attitude of being of service, of giving, helps in all situations.

Elizabeth Harper Neeld retrained as a grief therapist as one way of dealing with her personal loss. Every grief counselor of my acquaintance arrived at their profession for the same reason.

Remember my client who survived a pituitary operation, then set up a support group with others with the same problem? (p 21). This helped enormously in resolving her long-term grief for her father. Vlad, who felt suicidal after his family died in a car smash, tried to join the police, and ended as a dispatcher, saving the lives of others (p 64). And Dennis (p 21) took a traumatized teenager into his home precisely because of his traumatized childhood.

Think about your unique circumstances. How can you make this planet a better place, for just one person, or for people who share some aspect of your situation, or more generally? When you manage to do this, you will resolve your personal pain better and faster.

This is not instead of the activity of grieving, but a part of it.

Grief for a Child

Some people die before birth. Grief by the parents will be just as devastating as for a child who has achieved independent life. This is usually true even if the end of life was due to a deliberate termination.

Having an abortion can be a completely logical choice. My mother aborted two fetuses, because she didn't want to bring a Jewish child into Hitler's world. She decided to allow me to live when her doctor told her, "If you abort this one, that's it. Either a war baby or no baby." But many years later, when I was an adult, she told me of her grief for the two never-to-be-born children she chose not to have.

The same is true if the fetus is the result of a rape, or has serious defects, or any other reason for an abortion.

Children who die in infancy, for whatever reason, also leave a terrible hole in the hearts of those who had loved them during their short lives. And no, "You can have another one" doesn't help. As one grieving woman said, "But I love THIS one!" People are not interchangeable tokens.

We cope with this grief in the way as we cope with any other serious loss. In addition, there is a resource in many countries: <u>The Compassionate Friends</u>, an organization in which people who have lost a child before or a few years after birth counsel and support others who have experienced this tragedy.

If you are in this situation, check if your country has *The Compassionate Friends*. If not, maybe you can start one up? Remember, the more you give, the more you get, and the more you give, the more you grow.

Furbabies

...and other nonhuman children like horses are as special to many people as their genetic descendants. As I've told you, that's how Natalie felt about her cats.

There is a truly wonderful story in *The Guardian* by Joseph Earp: "<u>My Pet Rat Is Dying.</u>" Joseph had named his rat "Bob," so, hey, I have something in common with the little person. But rats are short-lived creatures, and Bob is now nearing the end of his life.

Here is a tiny excerpt,

> But here's the thing: Bob is my son. He is kind, cuddly, stubborn and wilful. Even people who don't like rats are moved by him. He's never even bitten anyone, except my friend Susie, who dared to talk to him when he was gnawing on a cucumber.
>
> More than anything else, Bob adores two things: his wheel, and me. (The order of those things is deliberate—I know he'd jump over my dying body for one more hit of the wheel, and that's fine.) For much of our time together, when I have picked him up, he has stuck out his little ratty hands and asked to grab my hair, which he will then carefully preen. When I googled this behaviour, I discovered it meant that he considered me one of his brood. So we are on the same page: I think he's my kid and he thinks I'm his, too.

So, when a pet like this passes on, the grief just has to be as severe as for a human occupant of your heart.

If the loss is the same for you, the grieving needs to be the same, too. And if a person you know has suffered this tragedy, you can offer support in exactly the same way as for someone grieving for a human.

Does The Loss of a Child Cause Divorce?

If you do a casual internet search, you will be told that 80% of marriages break up after the loss of a child, and that, in any case, more than half of relationships self-destruct. But when you look at articles based on research evidence instead of "everyone says that..."

you find it ain't so. <u>Divorce.com</u> states that "This misleading information has been widely quoted, including in reputable sources like *Psychology Today* and *Forbes*. It is important to acknowledge that these figures are inaccurate and should not be perpetuated." According to their information, it is less than half a percent.

A similar internet myth is that couples who lose a child divorce 80% of the time. The actual figure is 16%, which is much higher than for other couples, but then other sources of major stress like financial pressures and chronic illness also increase divorce rates. People have different ways of handling a major source of stress. One partner might shut down, while the other wants to talk. That mismatch can cause friction.

Suffering a tragedy of any kind gives us a choice: We can form a grieving team, or withdraw and attack. Losing someone you love, regardless of any other consideration, is the same.

We have already seen that when Jim and Margaret were caught up in guilt and blame, they split, and couldn't move on with their grief. Their breakthrough was mutual forgiveness, compassion, and support.

Supporting Grieving Kids

The angel of my infancy and early childhood was Aunt Janka. She was my grandmother's eldest sister; an "old maid" because she had a hump on her back. She became part of our immediate family when all Jews were forced into the ghetto in Budapest, and having one more person entitled us to another room in incredibly crowded conditions. When, thanks to my mother's brilliance, we survived the war, Aunt Janka stayed on as a family member. (If you are interested in the story, do read the award-winning biography of my mother, *Anikó: The stranger who loved me*. Actually, you can learn about grief in that book, too.) Here is how an unfortunate choice of words drove me into deep depression:

> I came home from school one summer day in 1951, and to my surprise Mother and Uncle Peter were there, but no Aunt Janka. Uncle Peter looked cranky and impatient. Mother and Grandmother had red eyes like they'd been crying. When mother saw me, she gave a little sob and hugged me. She said, "Oh, my sweet, Aunt Janka has gone away. She's no longer with us, but went to God."
>
> Now I understood why they were crying. How could I live without that little old lady? And how could she do this to me? If I was the child of her life and the child of her heart, how could she leave? If even she left me, then nobody really loved me, so I must be unlovable. If not even she loved me, then this would always be true. I was just unlovable. I was unlovable and nobody would ever love me. Mother didn't, and now Aunt Janka didn't.

Naturally, as I grew, I realized that Aunt Janka didn't "leave me" but had died. All the same, the little-child interpretation stayed on, poisoning my beliefs about myself. It is natural to want to protect a child by using euphemisms, but simple and direct is safer. My mother could have expanded on "Gone to God" with something like, "She has died but still loves you very much."

Lost but Found: A Boy's Story of Grief and Recovery by Lauren Persons is an excellent little book that will lead parents in the delicate task of explaining the death of a loved one to a child.

And if the child's grief is for someone who had died by suicide, *My Grief is Like the Ocean: a story for children who lost a parent to suicide* by Jessica Biles and Jillian Kelly-Wavering is an essential resource.

Part V: Finding Equanimity
Calm Acceptance, of Anything

In a way, all the book so far has been a prologue. Now at last I can share with you my way of dealing with every negative, from a minor inconvenience like dropping a sandwich to absolute catastrophe. This is the third reason I have coped well with my daughter's death.

I used to have a colleague, George Wills, who was prominent in Australian counseling psychology circles, a professor of psychology who had pioneered several new approaches to therapy. In a major speech at a conference, he told the audience of several hundreds that he had been diagnosed with the early stages of dementia. Warmly, emotionally, but without any signs of distress, he thanked all his many friends and admirers for their collaboration over the years, for electing him to positions of responsibility, and for their service in working to reduce suffering.

You can be sure, this was the result of a huge amount of emotional work on himself, not the waving of a magic wand. "OK, I am sliding into dementia, so what." No, he had to have reacted with "That can't be true. Let's look at your evidence again." and "Oh no! I'd rather die than become an incontinent old dodderer!" and other reactions of this kind. That's how I would react, initially.

However, George will then have used a set of tools to work toward such a level of acceptance that he could calmly tell a large audience of his colleagues about his misfortune. That's the reaction I would have progressed to, and that's how I have coped with major losses in my own life. I don't know what techniques George used, but I can describe mine.

In 2013, I noted bizarre beliefs and behavior exhibited by a new client and diagnosed her as suffering from Delusional Disorder

(Paranoia). Later, another psychologist and a psychiatrist both confirmed this diagnosis.

Almost invariably, I form an immediate, strong emotional bond with my clients. However, rather than coming to trust me, for our second session she chose to bring two of her friends along as protection from some imagined threat I posed, and after the third session, reported me for malpractice to the Psychologists' Registration Board.

It so happened that the person chairing the hearing had a known prejudice against senior psychologists. I was convicted of malpractice on completely spurious grounds, and given highly onerous conditions to fulfill.

Being 70 years old, I had considered retirement from time to time and now chose that instead.

For decades, the meaning of my life had been the joy of leading people from suffering to emotional wellbeing. I felt angry, unfairly treated, and as if a piece of my life had been amputated. No, it was not the loss of a beloved person from my life, but it was a major loss that led to grieving all the same.

Fortunately, I knew how I'd led other people out of similar reactions to far worse tragedies. As best I can recall, here are the tools I used, not necessarily in that order, and over and over as I went through the grieving process Elizabeth Harper Neeld described. Here they are for your use.

Anger Is a Choice

So is any other emotional reaction to anything. This is not an invitation to denial, but to facing up to it and dealing with it.

I've already quoted the Buddha, but it's worth repeating: "Anger is a hot coal you pick up to throw at someone. It is your hand that gets burned."

The alternative to anger is forgiveness.

I found it easy to forgive the ex-client. After all, her reaction to me was part of the condition she was suffering from. I did wish I hadn't been caught up in the crossfire of her beliefs, but hey, crap happens. Every time I got angry at her again, I could counter it with compassion. I am fortunate in having a rational view of the world, but "there for the grace of God go I."

The second source of anger I needed to deal with was "Not fair, why me." This is a frequent part of grieving, like "Not fair, why should John have died of cancer, and in such suffering, and left me alone!" (This is an exact quote from Rose.) And the answer is in the opening of this book. Rose was not alone. Most people lose loved ones as we go through life. And I was not alone. When I step outside myself for a moment, I see unfairness everywhere, and so, why not me? As I said, crap happens.

The man who'd led what I consider to be a kangaroo trial gave me far more trouble. His view of his job was to "protect the public from psychologists who break the rules of the profession." Fair enough, but psychologists facing him were guilty unless proven innocent, and the more senior and well-known the defendant, the more likely the conviction. So, to continue the military analogy (caught in the crossfire of my client's beliefs), I was merely another notch on his rifle butt.

In the head, I knew that being angry at him did me harm without the slightest effect on him, even if he were to find out about it. I imagine gloating might have been his most likely reaction. One thing would have been worse: to deny my emotion; pretend to myself that I wasn't angry. So, even years later, I occasionally acknowledged a flash of anger at the man.

However, the next tool helped.

Every Cloud Has a Silver Lining

Even Margaret and Jim found a silver lining from the terrible loss of their little son.

Without becoming obsessive, Margaret became very careful regarding safety issues.

When Jim asked for advice on how to avoid anything even vaguely like his error, I told him something I'd learned in the Boy Scouts. When facing anything, even an emergency, "pause and ponder." For one second, stop, consider the situation, and choose the best course of action. In the scouts, the example was: what would you do if someone fell head first into a fire? If you rushed in to help without thought, you might also fall in. Did his feet slip on something that will catch you, too?

These were small, practical habit changes, but the real silver lining for both was compassion and tolerance for each other. After their reconciliation, their marriage was stronger than before. In turn, that led them to be more compassionate and tolerant of everyone else.

If even they could find a silver lining, then surely I could, too, in my far easier situation. Perhaps you can, too, in yours, whatever it may be?

My silver lining was that after retirement I invested my time, energy and abilities in other ways that, combined, have provided more benefit to others than my psychotherapy practice had.

First thing was to redefine myself as a Professional Grandfather. The job specification is to strive for a tomorrow for today's youngsters, and a tomorrow worth surviving in.

We are officially in the sixth extinction event of earth, and when we unravel the web of life, we also fall through the hole. And survival is not that attractive in a world ruled by greed and hate, so the second part is equally important. That is, we need to work for a world ruled by decency.

Remember, the seventh magic bullet is meaning. This is the meaning that has kept me sane, thriving, and powerful, and if I were a vengeful sort of person, it would be my revenge against that kangaroo court judge. Because I have this purpose to live for, I genuinely don't care about him and his actions anymore—except hoping that he has also retired, so he cannot victimize other psychologists.

And once I couldn't be bothered to be angry at him, I was able to offer forgiveness and compassion. I don't know the man's history. Perhaps he, or someone he cared for, was badly treated by a helping professional, and without realizing it he was striking back? You know, "Do not judge me until you have walked in my moccasins for 100 days." Henry Wadsworth Longfellow is credited with saying, "If we could read the secret history of our enemies, we should find in each man's life sorrow and suffering enough to disarm all hostility."

So, how do I carry on being a Professional Grandfather?

Actually, the process started in 1999. In order to build up my practice, and because I enjoy being of benefit, I answered questions of despair on websites like <u>Queendom</u>. People soon tracked me down, and I got emails such as "I hope you can convince me not to kill everyone at my school," "I have no friends and even my parents hate me, I might as well be dead," and "I found condoms in my husband's pocket and we never use them and my world has collapsed." This has gone on to the present day, covering the full range of suffering. I have been blessed with the ability to heal with words. My answers have made a difference—and have gained me brothers and sisters, children and grandchildren all over the planet.

I started a blog that has made me a crowd of worldwide friends and is a major tool in my Grandfathering.

Having thought about how to be more effective, I realized that politics is the most important activity, so joined the one political party in my country that shares my values and aims: the Australian Greens. I also had time to become active in an organization that supports refugees, and to do volunteer work for a local service that cares for homeless people, drives people to medical appointments, feeds those who cannot afford food, and so on.

My writing has blossomed.

Once I deliberately considered this silver lining, my anger went. If I ever think about that hearing, and the un-hearing man who'd conducted it, I can genuinely shrug and smile.

When doing therapy, one of my tools has always been to ask a question like this: "Rose my dear, in what way are you a better person because of your grief for John?" She had made the not-fair comment in our first session. I asked her this in our second-last session, three months later.

So, when you are ready, ask yourself the same. How has your suffering made you into a better person? What is the silver lining to your grief?

Mindfulness-Based Grief Relief

Jon Kabat-Zinn's Mindfulness-Based Stress Relief (MBSR) is world famous, with a great deal of research evidence supporting its effectiveness in relieving suffering. I have used it personally when for years I was in the grip of ongoing, severe physical pain, and have taught it to many clients sent to me to deal with the effects of injuries, or conditions like fibromyalgia.

It is equally effective for emotional pain, whatever the cause.

So, while I was getting over my forced retirement, I applied it to that pain. You can apply it to your grief.

Naturally, by now you are an experienced meditator. If not, return to *The Power of NOW* (p 8), and get started. MBSR is an eight-week course, and whatever your circumstances, you will benefit from doing it. This is possible even if you don't have a facility near you. David Potter has established the <u>Palouse mindfulness center</u>, where you can do the full eight-week course online. It will equip you to deal with physical pain, the everyday annoyances of life, and severe emotional distress such as grief.

The final result of being competent at mindfulness-based stress relief is what I described in my little story, "<u>Heaven.</u>" However, note that it only works when you use it. I can go through days being a grumpy old man, then decide to switch back to being the best me I can be.

As you may have guessed from the name, the approach is based on mindfulness meditation. The very first exercise is to fully, 200% experience eating a raisin. You learn different ways of becoming mindful, including formal meditation practice, simple, easy-to-do yoga, and incorporating mindfulness into everyday life.

How will it help you with grief? How did it help me with my intense chronic pain, and distressing emotional reactions?

As you know, the essence of mindfulness is to allow all experience, simply returning to your current focus of attention. So, I was sitting with a client, and my focus was the complex activity of providing therapy to this person. When the severe, uncomfortable sensation in my hip intruded, I allowed it, rated it like, *Hmm, it's*

8/10 right now, then, through long practice, was immediately able to return my attention to my client.

When we are in severe pain, whether it is physical or emotional, we tend to identify with it: "I am this pain," as in "I am SO alone since Miriam's death!" or "I'll never be able to run again!" (negating the person's identity as a distance runner before the amputation), "I hate the way the fire has scarred me. I'd be better off dead!" (identifying with physical appearance), or... insert your example. (I've mentioned this earlier, on p 47.)

Rating something turns you into an observer. I cannot BE this pain and observe it. When I took a second to rate the discomfort in my hip, I automatically distanced myself from it.

OK, do the exercise. You are currently grieving, and from time to time, I am sure it feels as if the grief is swallowing the whole world, with nothing left. If you are fortunate enough not to be in this state right now, I am sure you can induce it. That takes courage, but you can't practice climbing out of a hole without descending into it.

Take a few deep breaths, focusing on your breathing. Then deliberately fall into the pit of deep despair. Calmly observe it and rate it out of 10, then return your focus to your breathing.

You can apply this method of acceptance, often called equanimity, at three levels:

1. I have an uncomfortable physical sensation in my hip. I accept it, and therefore I am not hurting.

2. However much I try, I cannot simply accept the sensation, so yes, I am hurting. I accept that for now, I am hurting, and it is OK and appropriate in my situation to be hurting.

3. It is too much and I cannot accept the pain. Life is not worth living like this. I accept that, for now, I am in despair. It is perfectly OK to feel despair, and this, too, shall pass.

And yes, I have sometimes been at level 3, and it did pass. Change is the only constant.

Strangely, achieving equanimity at one level often advances us to a higher one. After my hip operation, I was practicing walking with crutches. Got about a mile from home when the severe, uncomfortable sensation struck. I turned for home, and for a short while, managed to stay at level 1: "It's a wretched sensation, but it's OK." Then I made the mistake of estimating the remaining distance, and it was no longer OK. I was hurting, and in pain, and full of the miseries. *I'm only five days post-op, two days out of hospital,* I thought, and accepted the pain as reasonable. Once more, it stopped being a pain and became a severely uncomfortable sensation that was allowed to be there.

Mind you, there is a paradox. If you pretend to accept in order to move up the scale, you are not really accepting, and it is guaranteed to fail. The acceptance of wherever you are needs to be genuine.

All right, let's apply the concept to grief.

Suppose today is the three-month anniversary of your husband's death. All day, you've been barely managing to wait for your scheduled grieving time, and here it is. Looking at those lovely wedding pictures, you can hardly breathe for crying. The grief has you by the throat. You have accepted that he is gone, but the desolation is unbearable.

Ask yourself: "How bad is it out of ten?"

"ELEVEN! But this is a legitimate pain. I am supposed to feel this pain, and so it's OK to feel it."

It doesn't matter if this changes the rating. What matters is simply being in this moment, including the grief.

People with such severe pain that they need an implanted morphine pump have attended Jon Kabat-Zinn's MBSR course. At the end of the eight weeks, their physical sensations are just as severe, but they typically have the morphine pump removed. They no longer need it.

Same for grieving.

I don't know if George Wills applied this way of thinking to anticipatory grief for his intelligence. He may well have. You can apply it to whatever your worst problem is, right now.

Part VI:
Seeing the Big Picture
Why Are We on this Planet Anyway?

To me, this question is central to successfully resolving grief. Indeed, it is central to everything.

Remember when we discussed Elizabeth Harper Neeld's Choices of grieving? One of them was Solid Ground on page 20. The Choice was to find meaning in our loss, and to make sense of it by becoming a better person because of our suffering.

I made sense of my semi-forced retirement by becoming active as a Professional Grandfather.

I don't know yet how Natalie's death will make me into a better person. It is too soon. This kind of question is a long-term project, not one given to snap answers. Perhaps this book will prove to be the fruit of my loss. It is my hope it will be of service to many people.

And Finally...

As long as you live, a part of a departed person who has been significant in your life will stay with you. This applies even to those who had abused you. Resolving grief is possible—most people do it successfully—but suffering is a spur to growth, and you can make the choices that will lead you to becoming a better person.

Think of this little book as an instruction manual. It is a program for dealing with losses of any kind. You will benefit from it only by seriously considering each of my recommendations, and ACTING on those that fit your personality, beliefs and culture.

You can do it, and I am here for you. You can send me a private message via the Contact page of my blog "Bobbing Around." I am an old fellow, but as long as I am alive, my joy is to be of benefit to my family. And all sentient beings in the universe are my family. That includes you.

If you have bought this book, thank you. I have an ongoing policy of making the gift of a free electronic copy of any of my other titles to anyone who sends me proof of purchase of one of my books. A review qualifies as proof of purchase.

And if you have found this book to be of benefit, please spread the word about it. I want to be of service to as many people as possible, and that means they need to find out about it.

I offer you my work with metta. What does that mean?

"I wish for you to be contented, feeling good, free of suffering of any kind. I don't need anything in return, except the knowledge of being of benefit to you."

Bob Rich

August 2025

References

Earp, Joseph *My pet rat is dying*. https://www.theguardian.com/commentisfree/2025/mar/14/my-pet-rat-is-dying-i-cant-stop-thinking-about-all-the-things-he-taught-me

"Eaten Fish" https://eatenfish.com/

Frankl, V. E. (1946) *Man's Search for Meaning*. Currently available from Beacon Press, 2006.

Funchess, W.H. (1997) Korea POW: A thousand days of torment, November 4, 1950-September 6, 1953, self-published.

Harper Neeld, Elizabeth (2013 reprint) *Seven Choices:Finding Daylight after Loss Shatters Your World*. Grand Central Publishing.

Kübler-Ross Elisabeth (1969). *On Death and Dying*. Routledge.

Kübler-Ross, Elisabeth. (1997) *Death: The Final Stage of Growth*. New York: Simon & Schuster.

Long, J. (2014) Near-Death Experiences Evidence for Their Reality. *Missouri Medicine*, 111(5): 372–380

Mazari, N. (2017) *The Rugmaker of Mazar-e-Sharif*, Wild Dingo Press, Melbourne, Australia.

Oelklaus, Nancy (2023) *A Love Story*. https://www.amazon.com/Love-Story-Transformative-Power-Twelve/dp/B0CFWSCM3T/ref=sr_1_1

Pak, C. (2017) *Transcendence in Resilient American POWs: A Narrative Analysis*, Ph.D. dissertation submitted to the Faculty of the School of Theology and Religious Studies of The Catholic University of America.

Persons, Lauren (2020) *Lost but Found*, Loving Healing Press.

Raab, Diana (2024) *Hummingbird*, Modern History Press.

Rich, R. (2011) *Anikó: The stranger who loved me*, Anina's Book Company, circulated by Loving Healing Press.

Rich, R. (2013) *Ascending Spiral: Humanity's last chance.* Modern History Press

Rich, R. (2019) *From Depression to Contentment: A self-therapy guide.* Loving Healing Press.

Rich, R. (2021) *Lifting the Gloom: Antidepressant writings,* Loving *Healing Press.*

Rich, R. (1999) *The Travels of First Horse*, Anina's Book Company

Sullivan, T. A. "Escorting the Dead" blog https://taslookingglass.wordpress.com/2021/10/23/suicide-and-the-afterlife/

Wood, David Letter to the newly bereaved https://www.compassionatefriends.org/blog/letter-to-the-newly-bereaved/

From me to you, online

Please go to http://bobswriting.com/glinks.html for a list of links.

About the Author

Bob Rich, Ph.D. earned his doctorate in psychology in 1972. He worked as an academic, researcher and applied scientist until "retiring" the first time at 36 years of age. Later, he returned to psychology and qualified as a Counseling Psychologist, running a private practice for over 20 years. During this time, he was on the national executive of the College of Counselling Psychologists of the Australian Psychological Society (APS), then spent three years as a Director of the APS. He was the therapist referrers sent their most difficult cases to.

Bob retired in 2013, but still does pro bono counseling over the internet. This has given him hundreds of "children" and "grandchildren" he has never met, because many of these people stay in touch for years. His major joy in life is to be of benefit to others, and now he wants to be of service to people suffering a serious loss.

You can get to know him well at his blog, *Bobbing Around*, https://bobrich18.wordpress.com

* * *

Please remember to visit **bobswriting.com/glinks.html** There you will discover more than two dozen complementary short pieces in the form of fiction, personal memoir, and self-help vignettes that bring you a deeper understanding of grieving and its nuances.

From Depression to Contentment: A Self-Therapy Guide is a course of therapy in your pocket. You can be your own therapist, changing the way you see yourself and your world. Not only does this save lots of money, it also is 100% confidential. The book starts with first aid, provides an understanding of the nature and causes of suffering, instructs you in research-based techniques for dealing with your problems and, finally, teaches you an actual cure for depression.

- Every tool in this book is based on research, but presented in an easy to understand, easy to apply manner.

- With homework assignments, you will find your inner strengths, uncover the true source of happiness and develop great resilience.

- Learn how to put the philosophies of all great religions to practical use, even if you are an atheist.

- This program can help you start a new life -- one of meaning, positivity and purpose.

- Unlike instructional books, this book is not only useful but also enjoyable.

"If you're depressed and need someone who 'gets' you, who has been there and who can walk you through the journey toward a life worth living, then *From Depression to Contentment* will be your new best friend. Bob meets you where you are and can lead you home to yourself."

—Petrea King, CEO and founder of Quest for Life Foundation

From Loving Healing Press

A companion volume to Bob Rich's popular *From Depression to Contentment: A Self-Therapy Guide,* this little book is a collection of short stories and essays, each with a brief discussion that reveals a path to a good life. If you like a clearly laid out map to contentment, regardless of your circumstances, it's in *From Depression to Contentment.* If a ramble with surprising twists and turns is more your thing, that's *Lifting the Gloom.* And actually, the two go together like main course and dessert. Among the essays and excursions you'll find are:

- Laughter: the best antidepressant of all
- Defeating the Blood-Red Dragon: the legacy of childhood trauma
- Armor-coating our kids: become a great role model
- A Lucky Break: how to cope with anything
- Labels: us and them
- Plant Something Beautiful, Feed it with Sunshine, Water it with Love
- Buddhism concepts: equanimity is your friend
- Forgiveness is not just for other people
- The More You Give, The More You Grow
- Where Did You Put Your Attention?
- and more!

From Loving Healing Press

www.ingramcontent.com/pod-product-compliance
Lightning Source LLC
Chambersburg PA
CBHW021115130726
47988CB00003B/1035

* 9 7 9 8 8 9 6 5 6 0 5 1 7 *